T0278357

CONCORD'S
WRIGHT TAVERN

AT THE CROSSROADS OF
THE AMERICAN REVOLUTION

TOM WILSON

THE
History
PRESS

Published by The History Press
Charleston, SC
www.historypress.com

First published 2024

Manufactured in the United States

ISBN 9781467157377

Library of Congress Control Number: 2024937568

This book is dedicated to all those who believe in democracy
And to my wife, Martha; sons, Rob and John; and grandsons, Asher and Ezra.
Learn from our history and help us build a more perfect union.

CONTENTS

FOREWORD

Wright Tavern" is a misnomer. Amos Wright, the barkeep in 1774–75, was only briefly associated with the alehouse that still bears his name, and the building, in turn, was a drinking establishment for only a portion of its long existence. Even during its fifteen minutes of fame, it was known as "Mr. Taylor's house, by the Sign of the Elephant."

The tavern's claims to notice are modest. It enjoyed intermittent success as an inn for the traveling public. The business originated in 1747 as a public-spirited effort to improve the look of the town common, and it benefited from the patronage of local leaders, who conducted official proceedings there—and ate and drank at the taxpayers' expense. The subsidies continued to 1776 but could not guarantee profits. For one thing, the business faced stiff competition. Concord supported five public houses at mid-century, with three in the village. A quarter-century later, on the eve of the battle, there were nine—one for every forty-four men of drinking age. With pubs dispersed in the countryside and concentrated in the center, no one was ever far from a place to drink. Running a tavern was costly. Two proprietors mortgaged "Wright Tavern" to raise operating capital, one of whom died insolvent. During its heyday as an inn, the enterprise on the common went through four changes of ownership. From late 1775 to 1792, it belonged to an absentee owner in Charlestown, Massachusetts, who leased it to a changing crew of managers.

Amos Wright came to the bar honestly enough. His family ran a tavern at its large farm on the main road northwest of the center. His father,

Lieutenant Joseph Wright, was a pillar of the political establishment, serving as selectman for a decade, and at his death in 1755, seventeen-year-old Amos received a substantial bequest. A decade and a half later, he was a middle-aged married man with a wife and four young children to support and few means to do so. On the tax rolls in the early 1770s, he appears as a landless laborer with only a cow to his name. He was evidently living on the 114-acre Wright homestead in May 1773, when the property, including the tavern, was advertised for sale. It was time for a change. Already licensed to sell drinks, Wright signed on as landlord of the public house in the village now owned by Daniel Taylor, and though his tenure was fleeting, it was fateful. Through a quirk of fate, his name would endure in the annals of the town.

Ironically, on April 19, 1775, Amos Wright was hardly the man of the hour. His tavern briefly served the Patriot cause as the rendezvous of the local militia. Then it was taken over by British officers under Major John Pitcairn. Even as the unwilling base of the British Regulars, the inn was not alone. Colonel Francis Smith, the commander of the expedition to Concord, made his headquarters in the Jones tavern, operated by the son of the merchant who had originally built "Wright Tavern." In the anecdotes of the day, this newer enterprise takes precedence.

Wright's business will forever be remembered as the place where Major Pitcairn supposedly inserted a bloody finger in his brandy and pledged to "stir the damned Yankee blood" by nightfall. On Main Street, Ephraim Jones is a hero of the day. At his establishment on the common, Amos Wright is invisible. On April 19, Mrs. Daniel Taylor was in the barroom when the Redcoats barged in. In her fright at the intrusion, the proprietor's wife noticed four musket balls lying in plain view and impulsively hid them in her pocket. She then served the unwelcome guests. When it came time to settle the bill, Lydia Taylor unwittingly handed over bullets rather than coins. "Madam, what do you do with those balls?" asked one officer. "Sir, I would use them in a Firelock if I had one." The story of her defiance was preserved for posterity. If Amos Wright was present, no one took note.

Nor did that public house leave much of a legacy. It ceased to be a drinking place in 1792, when the building was converted into a bakery, as well as a residence. From the 1830s on, it devolved into a variety of low-end uses, including a livery stable, a manufactory of cheap goods and an illegal liquor seller. Through all these phases, nobody ever decried the popular disregard for the *historic* tavern. In the 1880s, concerned about the run-down, disreputable state of the building, so close to the Unitarian house of worship, Reuben Rice and Rockwood Hoar bought the property and turned its management over to a respectable body of First Parish trustees. Just as the tavern had originated as an improvement of the landscape, so it was saved for a similar purpose. Together, the meetinghouse and alehouse would present an attractive gateway to the town. Here was a far-sighted gift to future generations. But it was not an act of *historic* preservation.

And yet there are those who treasure Wright Tavern for its Revolutionary antecedents. The public house will always be associated with the Massachusetts Provincial Congress, which assembled in the First Parish meetinghouse in 1774–75 to resist Britain's takeover of the colony's government. Insisting on their long-established right to self-rule, the Congress, representing most towns in the Bay Colony, proceeded to seize the reins of government. In "Wright Tavern," the leaders of the rebellion hammered out their plans and made ready for the confrontation with the King's troops that everyone knew was coming but still hoped to avoid.

It was fitting that schemes of resistance were concocted at taverns. In the seventeenth century, public officials feared drinking places as potential sources of social disorder. "When drink gets into the brain," advised Reverend Increase Mather, "then out come filthy songs. Where there is rioting and drunkenness, there is wont to be chambering and wantonness." Yet taverns were also necessary to facilitate movement, commerce and public life. So, the Puritans permitted inns but controlled them tightly. In the eighteenth century, the authorities released their grip, expanded the number of licensees and approved all sorts of individuals, from the propertied to the impoverished, to be purveyors of strong drink. By the second half of the eighteenth century, as Concord's record shows, public houses rapidly spread across the land. In rural neighborhoods and town centers, people could easily find places to gather, read the latest newspapers and pamphlets from Boston and beyond, discuss current controversies with neighbors and build up what would come to be known as "public opinion." The coming of the American Revolution is often attributed to the vital agency of newspapers and the press in informing and mobilizing the people. However, public houses were also parties to this revolutionary mobilization, thanks to the democratization of licensing.

Wright Tavern was truly an ordinary (i.e., a tavern where public meals were provided at a fixed price). It was not particularly distinguished for its bill of fare. No one has passed down memories of its food or drink or relished tales of the eccentric men or assertive women behind the bar. Amos Wright, for all his troubles, is a nonentity. Yet he performed a critical service to his contemporaries in maintaining a space in which the American Revolution could gradually take shape in discussions about rights and liberties and the requirements of government based on popular consent. Here, the subjects of George III began to transform themselves into citizens of a new republic. In Wright Tavern, as in the First Parish meetinghouse, we can glimpse the beginnings of a civic culture that has underpinned our public life for centuries but seems to be faltering in a digital age marked by intense political polarization. It is a place not for nostalgia but for reflection, for considering what ordinary people can accomplish and for taking inspiration from their example.

Like the buildings preserved by the National Park Service along Battle Road, Wright Tavern has endured over the centuries, through good times and bad, as a witness to Concord's critical role in sparking the War of Independence and making the American Republic. It is integral to the historical landscape of a community that has long taken its civic identity from that decisive moment two and a half centuries ago. Cheers!

—Copyright by Robert A. Gross
Concord, Massachusetts

AUTHOR'S NOTE

Imagine this description by a Concord Minuteman on the morning of April 19, 1775:

It was a cool, crisp, clear day, this April 19, 1775. I woke shortly after 2:00 a.m. when I heard the bell from the townhouse. I got up quickly, dressed and grabbed my musket and supplies. I headed to the Amos Wright's Tavern, for this was the rendezvous point when we heard the alarm. Dr. Samuel Prescott had arrived in Concord shortly before and woke the custodian at the townhouse to sound the alarm bell. We all knew what this meant. The British Redcoat Regulars were on their way to Concord.

As we gathered in and around the tavern, we all knew that this day would come, and we felt anxious but prepared. Everyone knew it was just a matter of when, and now this was going to be that day. We learned from Paul Revere, who came to Concord a few days earlier, that British Major General Thomas Gage would send troops to Concord. They were going to search and seize munitions that we had stored all over the town, and what else, we did not know.

We spent the last several days moving and hiding our supplies. More men came walking into Concord Center with their muskets at the ready. I saw some friends from Acton and Lincoln, and we smiled but were serious about what was coming. The cool wind blew softly and muffled the conversations as we gathered around the tavern. Lights were starting to appear all over the town as people woke.

I entered the tavern and found Reverend William Emerson; Colonel James Barrett, our senior officer; and Major Jonathan Buttrick in intense discussion. By now, a few hundred men were congregating in and around the tavern. We learned from Reuben Brown, who had just returned from Lexington, and thought a battle had ensued there, although he came back before it had started. The British Regulars were now on their march to Concord. Buttrick and Barrett both knew that at this point, we would be heavily outnumbered. Should we engage the Regulars now and protect our town, or wait for the reinforcements of the more militias from Sudbury, Chelmsford and other surrounding towns? Today is going to be a day that will be remembered.

Chapter 1

OVERVIEW

In the center of Concord, Massachusetts, there is an iconic building built in 1747 with a unique and enduring history. This building is known as the Wright Tavern, and this is its story. It is the site of two significant events at the founding of the United States and served an important role in the formation and development of colonial Concord. Throughout its life, the Wright Tavern has witnessed many events and has experienced many uses. First Parish in Concord, a Unitarian Universalist congregation descended from a Puritan Congregationalist church and founded in 1636, currently owns the building. It was sold to First Parish in 1885 because the owners, Judge Ebenezer Hoar and Reuben Rice, knew it needed to be preserved and they thought it could provide additional income to the church. They were also concerned that it could become rundown and a disreputable drinking establishment. First Parish has maintained and operated the building since then and is looking to create a new chapter in the life of this historic building.

Over its history, the building has been a tavern, inn, bakery, bookseller, saddler, men's hair product manufactory, gift shop, Shaker furniture store, offices for an architectural firm and many other uses. It stands as a witness to the transformation of Concord from a frontier farming community, one of the earliest English settlements in North America twenty miles west of Boston, into a bustling commercial center and a suburb for commuters. Over its history, the occupants of the Wright Tavern have reflected many of these changes.

This is not the first book on the Wright Tavern. In 1835, Lemuel Shattuck, who moved to Concord in 1821, published *History of Concord*. He interviewed surviving participants of the Battle of Concord and became fascinated with the stories of the Revolutionary era and the growth of the community. In this book, he refers to the building as Wright's Tavern, and the name stuck. He became a leader in the school system in Concord. Then, in 1901, George Tolman published a book titled *Wright's Tavern*. Tolman was the curator at the recently formed Concord Antiquarian Society, which ultimately grew to become the Concord Museum. The museum offers visitors an extensive collection of artifacts, exhibits and art that trace the history of Concord and the United States. Of particular importance in the museum is one of the lanterns that hung in the North Church as a signal to the network of riders that warned communities about the march of the British Redcoats to Lexington and Concord.

The Wright Tavern has been closed to the public for most of the last forty years and has been used for commercial offices. The Wright Tavern Legacy Trust was established in 2021 to oversee the restoration, renovation and renewal of the building so that it can take its rightful place in telling the history and stories of Concord and the founding and development of our country.

This book is the story of the Wright Tavern, covering its history, ownership, uses, the evolution of the Concord community and significant events. The Wright Tavern is undergoing significant development. This book also describes the next chapter in the life of this important building in America's history. While this book has an ending, the life of the Wright Tavern continues. Perhaps at some time in the future, someone else will provide a sequel to this book and tell more about how the Wright Tavern has evolved as our society and lives change. So, let's travel through time and explore the life and experiences of this historic building and its environment, which reflect the changes in our society and the principles we cherish. Enjoy the journey.

Chapter 2

HOW IT BEGAN

The area now home to Concord and many surrounding communities was long settled by Indigenous people. The area was known as Musketaquid, which references the grasslands and rivers running through these lands. For over 12,000 years, Indigenous people roamed and settled in this area as sheets from the ice age began melting. The arrival of the Nipmuc people predates written records. They lived primarily west of what is now Boston and as far as the Connecticut River Valley. Freshwater rivers were abundant and provided much-needed water, fish and attraction to the wildlife living in the area. The region was plentiful with moose, giant beavers, caribou and other animals, and the rivers and ponds teemed with salmon, eels and other fish. The Nipmuc Nation lived mostly peacefully for over five hundred generations. They were hunter-gatherers and developed a system of governance with a tribal council and a succession of leaders, a code of ethics and myths. They were the people of this land.[1]

Over time, the Nipmucs settled into communities and started farming and adapting to the changing seasons. In the 1600s, the population grew to over fifteen thousand, and they lived primarily in central Massachusetts, Connecticut and Rhode Island. They lived as a community with no concept of private landownership or the accumulation of personal wealth and property. While there were periodic skirmishes with other tribes, there were also many intermarriages between the surrounding tribes (i.e., Penacook, Wampanoag, Pocumtuck).[2] The area around Concord was particularly important because of its multiple rivers and ponds and the hills by which they could view the countryside and protect the community. All this was about to change as the white newcomers from England and other nations "discovered" this open land. By approximately 1650, over 90 percent of the Native population, with no existing immunities, died of smallpox and other diseases introduced by English immigrants. Many others were sent into West Indian slavery or died in forced residence on Deer Island.

The English came to this land for many reasons. The Puritans wanted to create a community with a theocratic government based on their religious teachings (under the leadership of John Winthrop). Others saw opportunities to promote trade and colonize New England. Others thought they would find gold and silver as the Spanish had done in Central and South America. In the mid-1600s, thousands would be arriving, so that by the mid-1640s, the Massachusetts Bay Colony had a population of twenty thousand settlers.[3] Most settled on the coasts of the Atlantic, but they gradually started moving farther west. They would often utilize the abandoned villages of the Indigenous people and help themselves to the crops and open lands.

In September 1635, the General Court of Massachusetts Bay Colony gave a grant of land to settle a new town on the site of the former Indigenous people of the Musketaquid. This group included Reverend John Jones and his large family; Reverend Peter Bulkeley and his wife, Grace, and three young sons; and Simon and Mary Willard and their two daughters. This was the first community settled beyond the sight and scent of the sea. In testimony to Puritan ideals, the new town was called Concord, which means "in harmony between peoples."

Peter Bulkeley, a minister educated at the University of Cambridge in England, fled the religious repression of the official Anglican Church in his native England. Besides religion, Bulkeley brought with him the feisty tradition of English politics and his inherited wealth. His ancestor, the Earl of Winchester, was one of the twenty-five barons who imposed the Magna Carta on King John in 1215. Several centuries later, Bulkeley's descendants in Concord include Reverend William Emerson, also known as the Patriot Preacher, and Ralph Waldo Emerson, an author, lecturer, abolitionist and leader in America's transcendentalism movement.

Sherblom, in *Concord Stories*, reports that the late 1600s saw a dramatic rise in the standard of living in Concord. In the early and middle parts of the century, Concord had a low standard of living in comparison to those living in England, where most of the inhabitants were from. It was heavily agricultural and subsistence-based; most commerce was twenty miles away in Boston. By the mid-1700s, economic times boomed, as did the population.

Concord's population grew from 480 in 1680 to over 1,500 by 1760. People moved to Concord because of its job opportunities, fertile open land for farming (taken from the Indigenous people) and growth as a town on the perimeter of civilization.[4]

After Bulkeley died in 1659, his land (comprising thirty-one acres) in the center of Concord was conveyed to Captain Timothy Wheeler and his cousin George Wheeler. Following Captain Wheeler's death in 1687, he bequeathed a large part of this property to the town for a militia training field and town schools.[5]

In 1636, the new settlers to Concord dammed the Mill Brook to provide water power to a newly built gristmill. Over time, the dam created problems upstream and started eroding the area where the militia trained. The militia members were citizens of the community and provided protection for the village. Also, the mill's proprietors used their privileges to take sand and gravel out of an area around the pond to strengthen their dam. This left a very unsightly and dangerous gravel pit near the meetinghouse. Consequently, a committee was selected at the town meeting on May 18, 1747, and charged with finding someone to address this issue and negotiating a deal. The town wanted to find someone who would fill this hole and protect the training grounds. Captain Ephraim Jones became that person.

On June 2, 1747, the Town of Concord, Massachusetts, sold thirty rods (about one-quarter of an acre) near the militia training grounds to Captain Ephraim Jones (1706–1756), a trader, merchant and captain in the local militia, for thirty British pounds.[6]

The transaction with Captain Jones was arranged for a public purpose. It was intended to shore up the ground and prevent the training field from eroding. Jones, in turn, would benefit from the inn he erected on the site overlooking the pond. He fulfilled his promise. By August of that year, he had built a large frame house to live in on this property. As was common, taverns were a combination of residence and public alehouse. It was an important location next to the town's meetinghouse.

The front of the Wright Tavern.

Captain Jones lived there for only four years, until he was forty-five years old. He was very active in Concord's government, serving as a selectman (the town governing body) and the town clerk. A land surveyor, he was on the committee that established the town boundaries and assisted in laying out the roads. He was a captain in the militia, and after completing the construction of his home, he operated a tavern that furnished rum and other beverages to the townspeople and travelers to Concord. He was also chosen to be the "ringer of the bell" in the meetinghouse (and became its sexton) next to his new home.[7]

On November 25, 1751, Captain Jones sold the house and property to Thomas Munroe from Lexington.[8] Munroe had been operating a small inn. Captain Jones built another inn in Concord for his son (which became known as the Jones Tavern), but the captain died a few years later in 1756 and is buried in the South Burying Grounds in Concord. Munroe moved to Concord and quickly transformed this large home into an operating inn with his neighbor Jonathan Ball.[9]

Soon after the town was settled in 1635, the First Parish meetinghouse was built on the ridge across the street from the current location. It was under the leadership of Reverend John Jones and Reverend Peter Bulkeley. The church has been replaced three times, and it was moved to its current location in the early 1700s. The original meetinghouse did not have a steeple. A new church was built in 1791 with a steeple and then renovated and turned ninety degrees to face Bay Road (now Lexington Road).[10] The latest version was built in 1901 after a devastating fire. The bell that hung in the steeple now lies in the front yard of First Parish near the Wright Tavern.

Unlike today, colonial taverns were often located next to meetinghouses (since they were houses of worship, they became known as churches). On the Sabbath, these establishments provided refreshments for churchgoers who were distant from their homes. Alehouses were thus public utilities. Each benefited from the presence of the other. The Congregationalist church over which Peter Bulkeley and then his son Edward presided was established by law and funded by taxes. The community paid for the minister's salary and the operating expenses through taxes. This was clearly before the principle of "separation of church and state." The meetinghouse was unheated, with worship services often lasting four or more hours. So, breaks were often especially important times for rest, refreshments (both edible and spiritual) and conversations. Alcohol at that time was deemed to be good for your health. Located at the intersection of two main roads at the heart of the village, the tavern became a central point of gathering for both locals and travelers passing through.

Above: A lock on the front door of the Wright Tavern, taken in 2023 by Tom Wilson. *All rights reserved, Wright Tavern Legacy Trust.*

Left: A key to the front door of the Wright Tavern, taken in 2023 by Tom Wilson. *All rights reserved, Wright Tavern Legacy Trust.*

When the tavern that would later be referred to as the Wright Tavern was built, Reverend Daniel Bliss was the minister at the next-door First Parish meetinghouse. He was a high-energy, evangelical and controversial minister. Unlike his predecessors, he was educated at Yale (not Harvard) and was a deeply pious man. He was twenty-four years old when he assumed the pulpit in 1739 and remained there until 1764.[11] His sermons were often highly spirited and called for repentance and total faith in Christ. He held outdoor revivals, sometimes multiple days in the week. He also completely abstained from drinking alcohol and encouraged this with his followers. Reverend Bliss owned two or three slaves. He created even more social disorder when he baptized the enslaved John Jack and invited him to join the First Parish Church. Bliss died in 1763 of tuberculosis and was succeeded by his son-in-law to-be, Reverend William Emerson.[12]

Taverns became important foundations for growing communities. In 1656, the General Court of Massachusetts passed regulations that required towns to support the taverns. The town could be fined if it didn't support its local taverns. This, at times, created conflict between local Puritan churches and the taverns. While the Puritans did not favor drinking alcoholic beverages, they understood the importance of these places to building a sense of community. David Conroy, in his book *In Public Houses*, describes how taverns became the center of community life, business transactions and court proceedings. They often provided places for women and the poor to earn a living. At the same time, taverns were often highly criticized by the Puritanical clergy, and the community provided strict licensing and regulatory control over their operation. The forces created a complex relationship between different interests and the needs of the community.[13]

In the seventeenth century, the relationship between the tavern and the Puritan churches was strained, as many preachers felt that such drinking establishments would lead to unruly behavior, disputes and challenges to authority. Reverend Bliss was one such preacher. While Bliss was highly revered and respected, this did not stop many parishioners from enjoying the refreshments of the Wright Tavern next door.

The Wright Tavern, like all taverns in those days, was a place to receive refreshments; water was not healthy, so cider, ale, rum and other beverages were preferred. The favorite drinks of taverngoers were rum, grog (rum and water), rum toddy (rum, sugar and water) and flip (warm rum, molasses and an egg, stirred and cooked by a hot poker from the fire). Taverns also provided good food to their patrons. The food was whatever the proprietor had available. This usually included chicken, bacon and pork. Sometimes these foods were served in pies or on a plate with potatoes or meat pudding.[14]

Taverns became important elements of colonial America. Not only did they provide a place for travelers to spend the night, out of the weather of the countryside, but they were also important to the communities themselves. In colonial times, a person could perhaps travel only ten or twenty miles in a day, and so the Wright Tavern, being just twenty miles outside Boston, was a convenient place for people traveling west from Boston or on their last leg of a trip before reaching Boston. Travelers often provided important information about what was happening in other cities and areas of the country while they enjoyed refreshments with the townsfolk. The taverns served the same function as today's newspapers, television and social media, providing information about what was happening within the community and the broader world. Tavernkeepers regularly received newspapers and flyers from surrounding towns and shared them with their customers. Travelers and townsfolk alike would discuss and learn much of what was happening in the world.

Women were allowed in taverns but were excluded from the taproom. They often met in the adjacent rooms to play cards, talk with other women about the town's activities and enjoy both alcoholic and nonalcoholic beverages and food. They would frequently find ways to partake in the refreshments offered by the tavern. Many women were tavern operators, and the tavern was a good source of income for them. Most of these businesswomen were either widowed or single.[15]

Taverns in colonial America were the sites of many public activities in town, like trial courts (until courthouses were built), auctions, public whippings and the sale of slaves. There are no records of these activities at the Wright Tavern, but it had become a central part of life in this township. In those days, the town's selectmen did not receive a salary, but when they met in the tavern, the town paid for their refreshments. Because it was well-heated and had a good supply of food and drink, they met in this tavern often. The business of the town often required many hours of discussion and debate while enjoying an uplifting beverage and a good meal. Their business was also an important source of revenue for the tavern. This was very common in many communities in those days.[16]

Taverns were used as meeting places for gatherings with friends and family. They created a sense of community within the growing villages. People's homes were often small, so the tavern became like a living room to enjoy the company of friends. Many taverns in smaller communities did not favor a particular class, so they were a great democratization force. In larger cities (such as Boston and Philadelphia), certain taverns would cater to specific classes and clientele. As the communities developed, taverns expanded and offered other services, like dance halls, private meeting rooms, game rooms and more. They were often places where business was transacted. When a deal or agreement was made, it was often toasted with a drink. When a real estate transaction was made, the tavern often benefited from rounds of drink provided by the signatories.[17] And these establishments caused their share of trouble. Guests would sometimes drink too much, fight too much or engage in other disruptive behaviors to the community. The patrons could easily get stirred up by an effective orator and much drink.[18] As many of the Puritan and British authorities feared, taverns became places where people debated political issues, discussed issues with fellow patrons and recruited volunteers for the emerging revolution. Sam Adams frequently visited these taverns, including the Wright Tavern, to recruit members for his Sons of Liberty. Boston's Green Dragon Tavern was Sam Adams's headquarters for the Sons of Liberty; he was not alone in his quest for independence.

Even though the Wright Tavern was very popular, it faced much competition. Historian Robert Gross, in his book *The Minutemen and Their World*, reports that as the population of Concord grew, more taverns started popping up. In 1755, Concord had five inn-holders (including the Wright Tavern). Ten years later, it had seven, and by 1773, Concord had nine taverns. Concord had approximately one tavern for every forty male citizens.[19] It was expensive to operate the Wright Tavern, and Munroe needed capital. So he mortgaged the borrowing of £400 from Daniel Hoar, First Parish deacon Thomas Barrett, Jonathan Puffer and Tilly Mirick, pledging the tavern as security. At Munroe's death in 1766, the estate was hopelessly insolvent. Once again, the tavern had to be sold.[20]

The creditors recouped their investment by selling the property to Daniel Taylor. Taylor, in turn, pledged the tavern as security for a loan from merchant Duncan Ingraham. The sale required a standard mortgage to acquire much-needed operating money. Taylor conveyed the title with a cancellation clause specifying that if he did not pay the mortgage by a specific date (April 27, 1774), he would lose ownership of the property. Ingraham was strongly supportive of the King and the royal government. He was a wealthy ship captain and merchant in the Surinam (a Dutch colony) trade and gained considerable wealth as a slave trader. He advanced the money to Taylor to help him keep his public house going. Ingraham was a practicing Loyalist to the Crown, and Taylor was a Patriot dedicated to the rebel cause. This created a unique alignment in the history of the building: the tavern had a Patriot owner with a Loyalist creditor. The tavern would ultimately end up hosting both the Minutemen and Redcoats on April 19.

Taylor was able to make his payments, so the property was never transferred to Ingraham. Taylor owned it until December 20, 1775, and kept the inn going. It appears that a large part of this income for the inn was still coming from the meetings of the selectmen and other General Court sessions held in Concord, as well as from people who were taking breaks from the four- to six-hour-long services at the meetinghouse (which is now First Parish) next door. Unlike Munroe, Taylor was able to make the tavern into a successful business.

The Wright Tavern played many roles in the growing frontier community and faced many changes over time. While many tavern buildings were torn down as communities grew and habits changed, the Wright Tavern stands today in the center of Concord, Massachusetts. It was about to become an important place in American history.

Chapter 3

WHO WAS AMOS WRIGHT?

Amos Wright never owned the building that now bears his name. He was merely its proprietor on April 19, 1775, when the Redcoats came to Concord. Because of the significance of the events on that day and the work of the Provincial Congress six months earlier, his name became connected with this building. It wasn't until perhaps 1835 that this building became known as the Wright Tavern. Lemuel Shattuck, in writing about the history of Concord, used the label "Wright Tavern" as the location where the colonial militias rendezvoused on the morning of April 19. Perhaps after moving to Concord in 1821, Shattuck heard the local lore about this building and forever associated Amos Wright with it.[21]

Amos Wright was born in 1738 and was the tenth of thirteen children. He came of age in Concord when many fathers were no longer able to bequeath farmland to their children because there were too many sons and not enough land for all. The young were obliged to head west or north, where land was more plentiful and less expensive, based in part on the defeat of Native people in the Seven Years' War. But Amos stayed with his father, Lieutenant Joseph Wright, in Concord.

Amos's father died when Amos was seventeen. In this patriarchal society, the family cared for the teenage orphan and his younger brother Oliver, age fourteen. One of his uncles was Thomas Barrett, a mill owner and brother of Colonel James Barrett; he was also one of the supporters of Thomas Munroe's effort to keep the tavern operating. He served as guardian of the two boys until they reached adulthood. When Amos came of age, he inherited his father's "outlands" in Concord and a small stipend of money.

The legacy proved insufficient. Wright was not able to do much with the farm or make much of a living. By age thirty-three, he was married with four children and recorded in the town assessors' records as a landless laborer with only a single cow to his name. He apparently lived with his brother on their 114-acre Wright homestead. When it went up for sale, it was advertised in the May 13, 1773 issue of the *Boston Gazette* as the "valuable [Wright] farm…on the great road" to the west. The listing said that interested parties should contact Dr. Joseph Lee, one of Amos's uncles, or Amos Wright. According to Gross, in *The Minutemen and Their World*, Lee was a Loyalist and favored the King and Parliament during the war. When the land was sold, he and his family had to move.

It is not known exactly when Amos Wright became the innkeeper of the tavern; it was likely in March 1774. Working for Daniel Taylor, Wright was rich not in worldly goods but in progeny: he was the father of fourteen or

Smallpox burial grounds. Amos Wright is buried here in an unmarked grave. *All rights reserved, Wright Tavern Legacy Trust.*

fifteen children with two wives (Elizabeth until she died and then Abigail). This immense family likely lived on the upper floors of the tavern. According to George Tolman in his book *Wright's Tavern*, Amos Wright was referred to in town records as Captain Wright even though there is no evidence that he served in the militia. Wright never owned the building, but what transpired over the next several years would forever attach his name to the tavern.[22]

He remained the innkeeper until late 1775 or early 1776, when Samuel Swan acquired the building, approximately eight months after April 19. There is little information about what happened to Wright after the property was sold. He likely returned to farming and teaching, a job he had briefly held before turning to pouring drinks.[23] In 1780, he resumed his place behind the bar, and he was recorded as one of the nine licensed innholders in Concord when the license was renewed. One of his daughters was said to have been married in the tavern.

An outbreak of smallpox in Concord brought an end to Amos Wright's life in 1792. He is buried in the cemetery that memorializes the victims of smallpox of Concord. There is only one grave marked in this cemetery. It was for Sarah Potter. Historians believe there are about ten graves located in this cemetery. Amos Wright's name is listed on the grave registry at this site.[24] There is little known about what happened to his wife and very large family.[25] The cemetery is located at the corner of Fairhaven Road and Route 2 and measures about twenty-five by thirty-five feet. There is no stone marker for the final resting place for a man, bartender and innkeeper whose name lives in history.[26]

Chapter 4

FIRST MASSACHUSETTS PROVINCIAL CONGRESS

In the early 1770s, Boston became a hotbed of rebellion against the British government. This pressure grew gradually over the next ten years. Following the French and Indian War, which ended in 1763, Britain had a severe national debt of £114 million and made a policy decision to station military forces in North America.[27] Parliament decided to tax the colonists to cover many of these expenses. They saw the colonies as a growing source for raw materials and for trade to expand the business opportunities within the kingdom.

As the taxes and import duties increased, so did the protests against Parliament. Many of the colonists were loyal to King George III, but they felt Parliament was exercising excessive control over the colonies. The Boston Massacre, boycotts of British goods, the Boston Tea Party (December 16, 1773) and other rebellious actions caused the British government to crack down even more. Parliament demanded payment and restitution for the nearly $1 million of tea tossed into Boston Harbor and further initiated a series of acts to punish the colonials for their actions. These acts revoked rights guaranteed in the Massachusetts Bay Charter of 1691. These hated measures, denounced as the Intolerable Acts, became the talk of the taverns.

The Intolerable Acts included a series of legislative acts that increased pressure on Massachusetts. The first of these measures was the Stamp Act, which affixed a small tax on all legal and commercial papers (i.e., transactions). Although the Stamp Act was eventually repealed (approved by Parliament in March 1765 and then rescinded in March 1766), the colonists resented

Parliament for imposing these taxes with little involvement or interest paid to the colonies. However, to prevent a challenge to their authority, the King and Parliament declared in March 1766 that they had full legislative power over the colonies.

Next came the Justice Act, which eliminated the right to a trial by one's peers in a jury. The Quartering Act required people to provide food, drink and quarters to local British troops garrisoned in the community. Parliament passed, in March 1774, the Boston Port Bill, which closed Boston Harbor to commercial traffic and trading in punishment for the Tea Party. The port would not be reopened to trade until the colony reimbursed the East India Company for its lost cargo.

In 1768–70 and 1774, many colonists responded by boycotting imported British goods, including textiles and tea, and protesting in the streets. Occasional protests turned into violent mob actions, with the tarring and feathering of Customs collectors and other Loyalists. Except for Sam Adams and his Sons of Liberty, most colonists still professed loyalty as British subjects to the King, but their support slowly started to erode. There was an increasing challenge to differentiate the King from Parliament.

Concord was generally mixed, with many citizens remaining loyal to the Crown and others talking of rebellion. At the January 1774 town meeting, Concord citizens voted unanimously to boycott British tea. Economic times were getting harder for everyone. This was before the closing of Boston Harbor, but the boycott was an indication of the growing unrest even within quiet little Concord.

Then, on May 20, 1774, the British Parliament annulled the Massachusetts Bay Charter granted in 1691 by King William and Queen Mary. This was the governing document for the Massachusetts Bay Colony and established local representative rule as a governing principle. Then, the Parliament enacted the Massachusetts Government Act, which stripped the General Assembly (the lower house of the General Court and the governing body selected by the colonists) of its right to elect the upper house (Council) and stated that the members of the Council would henceforth be selected by and serve at the pleasure of King George III. It also banned the cities and towns from having more than one town meeting per year unless the governor approved additional meetings. This effectively eliminated home rule or governance of local affairs by the colonists. It would take effect on August 1, 1774. This act curtailed representative government, the rights of assembly and many liberties enjoyed by the colonies.

General Thomas Gage, commander-in-chief, colonies of North America, governor of Massachusetts.

Wiliam Legge, the second earl of Dartmouth and the secretary of state for North America, having given up his conciliatory approach after the Boston Tea Party, selected Major General Thomas Gage to be the new governor of the Massachusetts Bay Colony. Gage was already commander-in-chief of the military forces in the American colonies. Lord Dartmouth gave him full power to do whatever he needed to suppress the growing uprising in Massachusetts.

The colonists still regarded themselves as British citizens and were looking for ways to accommodate these changes. Efforts to find acceptable solutions were being promoted. But on June 17, the Massachusetts Bay Colony Assembly met to protest the actions of Parliament and proposed a congress of delegates from all the colonies in North America meet in Philadelphia in early September to develop a collective response to the challenges to British tyranny and taxes. This became the First Continental Congress in the Americas.[28]

By the summer of 1774, Major General Thomas Gage had become the most powerful man in the American colonies—even though his troops were confined to tiny Boston. He hated Boston. He saw the people of Boston as bullies, hypocrites and cowards. Fisher, in his book *Paul Revere's Ride*, said Gage saw that this problem was caused by the growth of what he called democracy.[29]

In late August 1774, about 150 delegates from throughout Middlesex County met in Concord to protest British measures. The delegates concluded that they should offer limited defiance to what they considered an unlawful authority. They also felt that a Provincial Congress was necessary to address "our present unhappy situation."[30] These meetings were held in the meetinghouse (now First Parish), and many took refreshments and made their decisions at the Wright Tavern during their time in Concord. In fact, the tavern became an important place for discussions, debates and decisions regarding the activities of the new Congress.

On September 1, General Thomas Gage appointed thirty-six members to the Governor's Council. This body would replace the upper chamber of the legislature, but the towns would continue to elect their representatives to the House of Representatives. Previously, the House selected the upper chamber, but this act took this right away. Eleven of the newly appointed members immediately declined the appointment, and many of those who accepted the post relocated their homes to Boston after receiving serious threats from the colonists. The colonists were upset about losing these rights to govern the colony. The governance struggles in the Massachusetts Bay Colony were heating up.[31]

In September 1774, the Court of General Sessions was scheduled to meet in Concord. Many of the townspeople in Concord were set on blocking that meeting. As ten justices arrived, including Squires Daniel Bliss and Duncan Ingraham, appointed only a year earlier, the crowd blocked their entry into the courthouse. Many of the townspeople were armed, and the justices feared for their lives. It is reported that the crowd acted with restraint but conviction. The justices then retreated to Ephraim Jones' Tavern on Main Street to determine their response (he was the son of Ephraim Jones, who built the Wright Tavern; this tavern no longer exists). They offered to meet but not to conduct any business. After some time, the townspeople, calling themselves the "Body of the People," rejected the offer, and the court decided to quit. No court sessions were held in Concord for another year.[32] Other counties followed suit.

Protests and a forming rebellion were increasing in intensity and frequency. On September 5, 1774, the First Continental Congress met in Philadelphia to discuss what to do about the unfair taxation and other grievances resulting from new regulations imposed on the colonies by the British government. The Massachusetts Assembly sent delegates to represent the colony (John Adams, Samuel Adams, Thomas Cushing and Robert Treat Paine). Their focus was on creating unity between the colonies. Twelve of the thirteen colonies were represented; Georgia did not participate because it was fighting a Native American uprising and needed British military support.[33]

The people of Concord struggled with this growing conflict between the governor and Parliament and the growing rebel cause. Many supported the protests, while others remained loyal to the Crown. There was intense loyalty to the King, but their issues were with the Parliament. This caused great struggles and confusion within Concord. The town was experiencing conflicts among the religious organizations and with the economic disparity in the town. The people of the town struggled with economic and social challenges. Civil strife occurred between friends in the community as well as within families. It must have felt like a civil war was brewing. The rebels or

Whigs increased their resistance to the Massachusetts Government Act. The Loyalists or Tories sought to remain loyal to the British government. The towns frequently acted independently, holding town meetings in defiance of General Gage's direct orders. The events over the next several months would result in major changes to how people saw this civil strife.

At the town meeting on September 26, 1774, Concord approved the establishment of a dedicated force, recruited out of the militia, that would "stand at a minute warning in case of an alarm." This was one of the first designations of the Minutemen; Worcester was also mustering its militias. The Concord town meeting approved the purchase of lead balls and gunpowder to create a war chest for the Minutemen. By January 1775, there were 104 Concord men, most of whom were under age twenty-five, in two Minutemen companies.[34]

A month later, on October 5, 1774, the Massachusetts Assembly met in Salem for two days and locked the doors to prevent Gage's order for their dissolution from being served. They met despite the direct orders from General Gage. They believed that Gage had no legal right to prohibit the delegates from meeting. They agreed to meet again—this time in Concord.

The assembly decided to organize itself into the First Massachusetts Provincial Congress. On October 11, 1774, meetings were held in the meetinghouse (now First Parish) and included 286 elected delegates. They elected John Hancock as president, Benjamin Lincoln as secretary and Henry Gardner as receiver general (treasurer). The Executive Standing Committee included Dr. Joseph Warren, Samuel Dexter, William Heath and Major Foster. Other attendees included Samuel Adams, Elbridge Gerry, Samuel Osgood and Artemas Ward. Reverend William Emerson served as its chaplain since he was the minister of Concord. Their presence intensified Concord's attachment to the popular movement. It also provided unexpected income to the innkeepers, especially at the Wright Tavern and local stores of Concord. Reverend Emerson opened the session with a prayer. Laborer Jeremiah Hunt served as the doorkeeper to the session.[35]

A few months earlier, North Carolina had created its own Provincial Congress, and while they discussed separation from British rule, they made no decision. Over the next several months, the Massachusetts Provincial Congress held meetings in Concord, Cambridge and other towns to avoid British confrontation. Their decisions reverberated throughout the American colonies.

In October, November and December 1774, the Provincial Congress met in Concord and Cambridge. The body exercised the powers of government

Left: John Hancock, Esq. *New York Public Library, Creative Commons CC0 1.0 Universal Public Domain Dedication.*

Right: Samuel Adams. *New York Public Library, Creative Commons CC0 1.0 Universal Public Domain Dedication.*

without any "civil constitution." However, forming a new government would be tantamount to a declaration of independence, and the Massachusetts representatives would not do so without support from the First Continental Congress in Philadelphia. In fact there was initially great resistance to move far without guidance from the Contiental Congress. As it was, the assembly in Concord and Cambridge had its work cut out for it to establish a governing body for the colony. The development of this Congress was a seminal event in the growing trend for self-government.[36]

The First Massachusetts Provincial Congress made several significant decisions. First, they focused on a limited agenda, but they needed to address the actions of Gage and Parliament. So they decided to take over the governance of the Massachusetts Bay Colony (excluding Boston) and develop a series of committees to address the needs of the communities. They said that they were operating under the authority of the 1691 Massachusetts Charter, although Parliament had rescinded it. Over time, this would become the de facto governing body for most of the colony. Soon after this decision, Hancock dispatched Paul Revere to the Continental

Congress in Philadelphia, informing the Congress that Massachusetts had essentially established America's first autonomous government.[37]

Second, they developed a series of committees that involved citizens' participation and representative self-government. While this may be considered an early form of democracy, voting rights were not extended to all. Only men over the age of twenty-one were entitled to vote; this excluded the poor, women, freed Blacks and slaves and all Indigenous people. They voted for representatives, and the government was still considered to be ruled by an elite governing class. This action seized power to govern the colony away from British control.

Third, the Congress took control of taxes. This was a key decision and treasonous. They declared that all provincial officers, including tax collectors, sheriffs and constables, were prohibited from paying any money to Harrison Gray, the colony's tax collector. Instead, they should give this income to the Provincial Congress. They required each town within the colony to create its own militia if they had not done so before. The companies would elect their own officers, and the Provincial Congress took control of the regiments. They used the tax money to support the acquisition of supplies for this effort. The Congress ordered the stockpiling of arms and munitions to support the building rebellion.

Fourth, they created and reinforced a series of committees to support their governance of the Massachusetts colony. The Committee of Safety was established to oversee the formation and oversight of the militia to protect and defend the province and supervise the procurement and distribution of munitions. The Committee of Correspondence communicated and coordinated resistance efforts with other colonies and committees within the towns. Other committees, including Supplies and Taxation, were created to provide governance to this newly independent colony. Finally, they developed a set of rules for a Continental army, which was important for several reasons. It meant that the colony was indeed going to create an army to support the rebellion, and it provided rules for governing each militia according to the same standards. These requirements were quite unusual for independent communities.[38]

One of the most interesting aspects of this Provincial Congress is that this group of men was literally forming a new government independent of a monarchy, military dominance or a guiding constitution. The original Massachusetts Bay Charter was founded on many of the principles of the Magna Carta (implemented in June 1215). This document stated that the King and Parliament were not above the law. It empowered the citizens with certain rights, which over the subsequent years began eroding away, especially in the American colonies. So this group of men sought to return the colony to a time when the government got its power from the governed, decisions were made by representatives of the people (at this time, they were white, property-owning males) and the government's purpose was to provide for the common good of all its citizens. However, this went further, and they figured out how to create an independent government based on these principles. Many of these principles were emerging throughout the American colonies, and when the Congress met in Concord, they were discussed and debated in the Wright Tavern.

Most people, even in Massachusetts, remained loyal to the Crown but felt that their treatment was unjust and indefensible. John Hancock and Sam Adams became fugitives and went into hiding to avoid getting arrested and sent back to England for trial. Many supported Hancock and Adams and resisted any effort to capture them. This rudimentary form of independent government served as the governing body over the colony until it adopted a constitution, and elections were held in October 1780.

The Provincial Congress struggled with the issue of slavery. Some of the delegates owned enslaved people or made their fortunes through the slave trade. The language of freedom to the slaves was growing and was regarded by many as dangerous. The issue grew because four slaves—Peter Bestes, Sambo Freeman, Felix Holbrook and Chester Joie—had sent a letter to the House of Representatives before it was disbanded by the Massachusetts Government Act. These men expressed a proposal that while the colonists were seeking to free themselves from the tyranny and slavery imposed by Parliament, why not "take our deplorable case into serious consideration, and give us that ample relief, which, as men, we have a natural right to."[39] They were asking for their freedom. The House of Representatives and the Provincial Congress decided not to take up the question, and so slavery remained an open issue in Massachusetts. The Massachusetts Provincial Congress did decide to bar the enlistment of slaves in the Massachusetts militias, but Black freedmen were permitted to serve. This is in spite of the participation of between twenty and forty slaves participated in the Battle of Concord on April 19, 1775.[40]

When the Provincial Congress met in Concord, the committees and Congress leaders met in the Wright Tavern to plan and manage the meeting's activities. This was an important source of income for Amos Wright, and the rooms in which they deliberated remain largely intact today. The Wright Tavern became a center where many of these ideas were deliberated and decided.

In November 1774, the Provincial Congress authorized the citizens of Concord to store a rising supply of food and armaments to prepare for a battle with the Redcoats. These were called "stores." This included twenty thousand pounds of musket balls and cartridges, 206 tents, iron cannonballs, fifty-one wood axes, twenty-four boxes of candles and twelve bushels of oatmeal. Townspeople also hid fifty-five barrels of beef, six hogs, seven loads of fish, eighteen caskets of wine, two casks of raisins, fifty barrels of salt and thirty-five thousand pounds of rice. These were hidden in fifteen different locations, including the townhouse. Supplies came in from surrounding towns. Because of its geographic location, typography and growing patriotic fervor, Concord became a supply depot for an anticipated revolution.[41]

The Wright Tavern (the name did not actually appear until the early 1800s) was likely the location where intense deliberation and discourse occurred, given its proximity to the meetinghouse where the Congress held its plenary sessions. Taverns were where many such heated conversations and arguments occurred. One can imagine that the townspeople were also engaged in many of these discussions. The events and activities during this Congress became important contributions to the formation of this new country. While similar discussions were occurring in other colonies, this Congress was one of the earliest deliberative and decision-making bodies.

While it initially began as a protest to the Massachusetts Government Act, the discussions in the Congress and the taverns evolved into a serious exploration of separating from the British Crown and establishing an independent colony. Most delegates desired to remain part of Britain; their issues were with the Parliament, and they remained loyal to the King. No one knew at the time where this would lead. For the entrenched rebels, this Congress set Massachusetts and other colonies on a path toward independence. It would not be long before these struggles would lead to the beginning of the Revolutionary War, in which all the colonies would unite behind the struggles that were blazing in Massachusetts. Following the Battles of Lexington and Concord in April 1775, the Second Continental Congress moved to adopt the Declaration of Independence in July 1776, only fourteen months later.

Chapter 5

THE REDCOATS ARE COMING

All these buildups of military stores did not go unnoticed by General Gage. He had several spies in Concord who fed him regular updates on what was happening in the town. Daniel Bliss, Esquire, a prominent attorney in Concord (and son of Reverand Daniel Bliss); Duncan Ingraham; and Dr. Joseph Lee were well-known Loyalists. While Bliss left Concord, both Ingraham and Lee remained after the war. However, the townspeople did not know that Dr. Benjamin Church, a member of the Provincial Congress, received large payments from General Gage for his detailed reports on what was happening in Concord and at the Provincial Congress.[42] Spies existed on both sides.

On Boston Post Road, not far from Boston and Concord (in what is now the town of Weston), was the Golden Ball Tavern. This tavern was a safe haven for the Tories, or those loyal to the Crown. It was operated by innkeeper Isaac Jones, a known "friend to the government." However, his loyalties fluctuated between the Crown and the Rebellion. While there were several attempts on his life and those of his family, Jones continued his innkeeping profession even after the war. There were carefully identified Tories or Crown-sympathizer taverns and inns in Marlborough and Worcester. Concord, and the Wright Tavern in particular, was regarded as an "arsenal of the revolution."[43]

On March 20, 1774, General Gage asked two British officers, Captain John Brown and Ensign Henry De Berniere, to travel to Concord on a secret mission to examine the conditions there. They traveled to the Golden Ball Tavern. When they arrived in Concord the next day, they stayed at the home of Loyalist lawyer Daniel Bliss. He welcomed them and showed them around the town. After graduating from Harvard Law School, Bliss moved to Concord in 1771 and became a property owner and an important figure in Concord. He remained committed to the Crown. It is likely but unknown whether the officers stopped to have a drink at the Wright Tavern. Since it served as one of the headquarters for the British Regulars when they came to Concord, it is likely Brown and De Berniere gave General Gage information about this tavern, as well as its central location on Bay Road and the center of this community.

Not long after they had arrived, Bliss received a letter warning him to leave town. The British officers were well armed and offered to escort him back to Boston. The three of them left shortly after receiving the threatening notice. At Bliss's encouragement, they traveled north through Lexington and Menotomy (currently known as Arlington) and found the road much easier and more open than the route the officers had traveled earlier. On returning to Boston, they shared this information with General Gage, who decided that his troops would travel through Lexington rather than the southern route through Weston on their mission to Concord.[44]

General Gage realized the revolutionaries were stockpiling arms in the event of a possible rebellion and felt that the best way to prevent the uprising was to confiscate the arms before they could be deployed. This would eliminate the Americans' ability to take up arms against the Crown. Though Gage waited for explicit orders from his superiors, he began devising his plan and preparing for the eventual mission.[45]

The orders to arrest John Hancock and Sam Adams, break up the Provincial Congress, and seize the munitions stored in Concord were issued on January 27 by Lord Dartmouth, the secretary of state for North America. They were sent by ship, but they didn't arrive in Boston until April 5, 1775. A copy of the orders was secretly sent by faster schooner and arrived in Marblehead on April 2, several days before the original orders reached Gage. This was a lucky break for the rebels. Upon hearing about these orders, John Hancock quickly left with his fiancée, Dorothy Quincy, and traveled to a friend's house in Lexington, Reverend Jonas Clarke, the town's minister. Sam Adams's wife went to their farm home in Braintree, and he headed to Lexington to meet Hancock a few days later. General Gage had not received the orders, so he was concerned about why the rebel leaders were fleeing Boston.

While these events were happening in the countryside, it wasn't until General Gage finally received his orders to stop the rebellion that he began the mission. Gage ordered several patrols of Regulars to go into the countryside to look for and arrest suspicious travelers connected to these rebel activities.[46] Dr. Joseph Warren, a Boston resident and a significant leader of the rebel cause, also heard about this order from the copy arriving in Marblehead or a well-positioned spy. Some believe that this spy was Margaret Kemble, General Gage's American wife, but others dispute this.[47] The news of the order reached the Provincial Congress meeting in Concord in early April. So they believed that a battle for their freedom was coming to Concord and about to begin.[48]

The Patriots (the rebels) in Boston soon witnessed much preparation by the Regulars in Boston. They also learned about the trip to Concord by the two British officers and concluded that the mission was about to be launched. On Saturday, April 8, Paul Revere traveled to Concord to warn the town's leaders of the impending military action. He returned to Boston, and the people of Concord started moving their munitions and supplies out of town and hiding them in old farmhouses and in the fields and surrounding communities. The Provincial Congress was meeting in Concord during this time and heard this news. They agreed to adjourn on April 15 for a period of three weeks, and its members quickly left Concord.

General Gage was reluctant to strike against the growing rebel militias without a larger force and had requested that Parliament send an additional twenty thousand troops so that he could implement the order. He only had about six thousand troops in Boston. He knew that the rebels were growing in number and were becoming well-armed. He also knew that many of the rebels were experienced fighters from the French and Indian War. But Parliament and Lord Dartmouth refused this request. With Lord Dartmouth's order, Gage had no recourse; he had to act. Gage's only recourse was to make this mission quiet, make the force appear significantly stronger than it was and act decisively and respectfully. He did not want to cause an overreaction by the country folk.[49]

Easter was on April 16 that year. Revere rode to Lexington to warn John Hancock and Sam Adams that the British were making ready for their march to Lexington and Concord to capture and arrest them and return them to London for trial and execution for treason. Following this meeting, he returned to Cambridge to alert those in his signaling network to be ready. Here, they devised the lantern signal from the North Church to communicate the beginning of the march to Concord to those outside Boston.

Around ten o'clock in the evening of April 18, General Gage gave the order for the British Regulars to cross the Charles River and start their mission from Phip's Farm (now Lechmere Point) in Cambridge. From there, they would take their mission to Lexington and then Concord. Their plan was to capture and arrest John Hancock and Samuel Adams, whom they knew were hiding in Lexington, and then go to Concord and seize and destroy all the munitions and militia supplies. The orders were known only to the commanders; the rank-and-file troops did not learn the nature of their mission until later in the day. The orders were given to Lieutenant Colonel Francis Smith and Marine Major John Pitcairn. The order also had a twist: the

British Lieutenant Colonel Francis Smith commanded British troops at the Battles of Lexington and Concord. *Wikipedia.*

soldiers were not to plunder the inhabitants or hurt or steal private property. Gage was concerned that such actions would create more outrage and trouble for his troops while in the countryside. He gave Smith a Concord map showing detailed locations of where many of the arms, cannons, and other supplies were stored.[50]

Between 10:00 and 11:00 p.m., several companies of British Regulars started boarding boats and crossing the Charles River. Shortly after this movement began, two lanterns were lit in the steeple of the North Church in Boston. Revere left Boston by boat to Charlestown to begin his journey to Lexington and Concord. William Dawes left earlier, about 9:00 p.m., at the request of Dr. Joseph Warren, and he successfully slipped through the British guards, crossed Boston Neck to Roxbury, Brookline, and Waltham, and headed off to Lexington.

The lantern lights glowed for only a short period so as not to be discovered by the British. Other riders who were part of the signal network devised by Revere saw this signal and left Boston and Cambridge for other towns throughout the region to sound the alarm. William Dawes, however, didn't stir the countrymen and focused on getting to Lexington to warn Hancock and Adams.[51] Revere arrived in Lexington at about midnight and swiftly went to the home of Reverend Jonas Clarke, where Hancock and Adams were staying. About thirty minutes later, Dawes arrived. After a brief time for refreshments at the Buckman Tavern, all men agreed that Concord

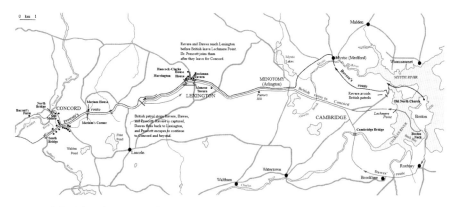

National Park Service map of Prescott's ride and march of the British Expedition on April 19, 1775. *National Park Service, Wikimedia Commons.*

needed to be warned, and so Revere and Dawes headed out to Concord. As they left, the Lexington town bell began to ring, which was a call to arms for the local militia.[52]

Dr. Samuel Prescott was leaving Lexington at about 1:00 a.m. for home in Concord when he came upon Paul Revere and William Dawes. He was leaving the home of Lydia Mulliken, his fiancée, who lived in Lexington.[53] He was twenty-three, and they had recently become engaged to be married. Unfortunately, the marriage never took place because Prescott was captured on a ship in 1777 and died in British captivity in a prison in Halifax, Nova Scotia. Dr. Prescott knew Revere and Dawes and was regarded as a strong friend of the rebel cause.

After briefly chatting about their mission, Dawes, Revere and Prescott started their ride to Concord. After a short ride, they approached what first appeared as two men on horseback. Then, suddenly, they were surrounded by a trap of British Regulars. In an instant, the three ran their horses in different directions as the Regulars yelled at them to stop. Revere headed forward but soon found himself surrounded by ten Regulars pointing their guns at him. He was captured and detained by these Regulars for several hours. Because he did not carry a gun that day, he was able to talk himself out of being arrested. He was left without a horse to find his way back to Lexington. Dawes's horse suddenly took fright, pitching him out of his saddle and onto the ground. Hurt, shaken and on foot, Dawes hid from the Regulars hunting for him and made his way back to Lexington. Dr. Prescott knew the territory, stone fences and backroads. He evaded the British Regulars and made his way to Concord.

Had he not met up with Revere and Dawes that night, the outcome of this day may have been very different.

The British Regulars patrolling the roads west of Boston did not know about the mission to Concord. They were simply under orders to halt, interrogate and arrest, if necessary, anyone acting suspiciously. They had no idea what the encounter with Revere, Dawes and Prescott meant to them, the British forces coming their way or the events about to unfold.[54]

It wasn't until about 2:00 a.m. that the British Regulars finally crossed from Boston to begin their march to Concord. General Gage wanted this mission to be done quickly, quietly and without notice from the townspeople. It turned out to be none of those things. After landing in a swamp in Cambridge, the troops slowly made their way to dry land, but their feet, trousers and jackets were wet and muddy. Most of the soldiers did not know where they were going and had only prepared enough food and ammunition for a single day. It was still very dark as they started their march on the road to Lexington and Concord.[55]

At about the same time the British began their march that morning, Prescott arrived in Concord. He found the caretaker for the townhouse, Amos Melvin, to sound the bell alarm and alert the townspeople of the British advance.[56] He then went to Reverend William Emerson's home, a known leader of the Concord Militia, to alert him personally. After that, Samuel Prescott mounted his horse again and headed off to Acton to alert other townspeople and militias to come to Concord. Prescott also asked his brother, Abel Prescott, to travel to Sudbury and other towns south of Concord to sound the alarm.

The Wright Tavern had been designated as the rendezvous place as part of the preparation plan. Reverend William Emerson was the first to arrive. Colonel James Barrett and Major Jonathan Buttrick, the leaders of the Concord Militia, and Reverend William Emerson gathered in and around the tavern to plan their response. It was a chilly morning, and it is likely that Amos Wright, the licensed innkeeper, or his wife opened the door and offered food and beverages to the militia officers. The militia furnished themselves with munitions and other supplies from a stockpile in the townhouse. They knew that many of the surrounding towns would be sending their militias to Concord. Should they wait for reinforcements or engage the British, knowing they would be heavily outnumbered? How should they protect their town? How should they address what was considered as the mightiest military force in the world moving steadily to their town?

Major Buttrick asked Reuben Brown, a local saddler and friend of the Revolution, to go to Lexington and come back with reports about the number of Regulars and any other news. Brown was a young, strong man who knew how to ride his horse fast. He quickly made the seven-mile trip to Lexington. As he entered the town, he witnessed the British Regulars entering the town and a long line of Redcoats on the road from Boston. The British officers ordered the Lexington militia to lay down their arms. After first standing firm, Captain Parker, the commander of the Lexington Militia, ordered his men to disperse and not to fire. Brown was convinced about what was about to happen, and as he started returning to Concord, he heard the firing of muskets and saw smoke rising from the village green.[57] Even though the British and the militia commanders had told their troops not to fire, someone did. Shots soon rang out; eight colonial militiamen fell dead, and the Regulars started charging. Confusion reigned before the British and militia commanders got their soldiers under control. Soon after, Lieutenant Colonel Francis Smith sent a rider back to Boston to ask General Gage to send reinforcements.[58] One can imagine that Colonel Smith realized this mission was going to be much more difficult.

Brown reported what he had seen to Buttrick, Barrett, Reverend Emerson and others. When Major Buttrick asked whether bullets were being fired, he replied, "I do not know." Then, he added, "But think it probable." Although the Concord Militiamen did not know if there had been a battle, they knew that war or peace still "hung in the balance."[59] They knew the Regulars were now coming to Concord, and they feared that soon Concord would experience what had happened in Lexington— or worse.

A small group of the Concord Militia went to Meriam's Corner, about a mile from Concord Center and the Wright Tavern, and saw the British troops marching in formation toward them down the dirt road from Lexington. Seeing what was coming, Colonel Barrett ordered his troops to take positions away from the town and up in the hills around Concord. Most moved to Punkatasset Hill just beyond the North Bridge, and others stayed closer to watch the British Regulars. The militia quickly took their positions in the hills and waited. This proved a wise move because as they waited, more reinforcements began arriving.[60]

On the hill across from the Wright Tavern, along the ridge that defined the Bay Road (now Lexington Road), militiamen waited for the British. They took their position near the town's tall Liberty Pole with "its flag waving defiantly in the western breeze."[61] The view must have been breathtaking. Over seven hundred smartly and menacing soldiers and sixty-six officers were marching in their red and white uniforms, muskets and bayonets glistening in the bright morning sun. The number of Redcoats was close to half the number of citizens living in Concord at the time. To the residents, the sheer numbers, bright and formal uniforms and fully armed soldiers coming into their town must have been overwhelming. One could hear the drums and fifes and the boots tramping and see the coming of danger.

Chapter 6

BRITISH REGULARS ENTER CONCORD

At around seven thirty in the morning of April 19, Lieutenant Colonel Francis Smith and Major John Pitcairn led their men into Concord village without encountering any resistance. The only people in view were women, children and some older men. Most able-bodied men had left the town and gone into the hills. The British Regulars were under orders from General Gage not to interfere with or disrupt anyone in the town, and they were ordered to respect private property.[62] They hoped not to repeat what had happened in Lexington. One could imagine what was on the minds of the people remaining in Concord as they watched hundreds of fully armed Redcoat Regulars enter their village.

The light infantry continued to walk along the ridge overlooking the town. Smith and Pitcairn hiked up the ridge from the town and saw the Liberty Pole. It is believed that this ten- to twelve-foot pole had a rebel flag flying from its top and was located on the ridge behind Reuben Brown's house. When British soldiers came upon similar statements of the rebellion, they would cut them down, so a group of light infantry left the main assembly and promptly cut down Concord's liberty pole. They then dragged the pole into the center of the town near the townhouse. This pole would later cause problems the British did not anticipate.[63]

The British officers moved quickly to set up a command center in and around the Wright Tavern. Amos Wright offered no resistance. Major Pitcairn established his headquarters in the Wright Tavern, while Lieutenant

A View of the Town of Concord, April 19, 1775, by Timothy Martin Minot, about 1825. *Concord Museum Collection, at bequest of Mrs. Stedman Buttrick, Sr.; Pi414.*

Colonel Smith established his headquarters in the Jones Tavern about fifty yards away.[64] Smith dispatched six companies (about 400 men) under the command of Captain Lawrence Parsons to go to Barrett's farmhouse, where spies had indicated significant arms were stored. Another company was dispatched to secure the South Bridge. They sought to secure the bridges from the militias gathering in the hills outside Concord. This would protect the Regulars in Concord so they could complete their search and seizure of munition and other military supplies. The British had maps and knew where to look based on reports from their network of spies.

After crossing the North Bridge, Captain Parsons realized that he might need an escape route, so he ordered Captain Walter Sloane Laurie to take the Fifth and Forty-Third Companies (about 115 men) to guard the bridge. Finally, Smith ordered his remaining grenadier soldiers, who were most of his men, to begin searching every home and store for military supplies for the rebel cause. They immediately took to their mission and started searching the town, knocking on doors and demanding entry. They were also anxious and wanted to get back to Boston as quickly as possible.[65]

About three hundred British Redcoat Regulars remained in Concord. A second battle was brewing in Concord, not a violent one, but one that rendered the mission of the Regulars mostly a failure. The defenders were the women and older men who could not take up arms against the Redcoats but had to use their wits and wisdom. There are many stories about the subtle civil disobedience and clever resistance of the townspeople to the Regulars in Concord that morning. Some were documented, and others

View of the Wright Tavern, part of a painting attributed to Timothy Martin Minot (1757–1837), 1825, oil on canvas, after work by Amos Doolittle, 1775. *Concord Museum Collection, at the bequest of Mrs. Stedman Buttrick Sr.*

were handed down through families and folktales to become popular legends. Many are based on facts, and others are no doubt embellished as the stories are told. The important message of these stories is that they tell what life was like during the brief occupation by the British Regulars and how the citizens of Concord and the surrounding town felt about this event. Their stories are important for us to understand the experience and actions of these inhabitants as they sought to defend the rights they saw ebbing away. These stories often had an emotional impact on the townspeople, militia and British Redcoats. As is often the case during times of great trauma, the story is not as important as the emotional impact and mindset they create. So, let's look at what supposedly happened in Concord on this fateful day.

There is a famous but often recanted story about the British officers soon after they entered the town. While at the Wright Tavern, Major Pitcairn is said to have stirred his hot-toddy drink with his finger and threatened to "stir the Yankee blood on that day." After the unexpected defeat of the British soldiers at the North Bridge, this became a favorite tale. It is also unknown whether the British paid for the drinks and meals served to them at the Wright Tavern. There are some indications that they rarely paid for their food and drinks since they set this building up as their headquarters during the siege. In many cases, it was apparent that only the officers offered compensation for the services of the townspeople.[66]

There is a story about a British soldier who removed a large Bible from the meetinghouse and burned it in the town center, but other reports indicate it was just stolen. Whether this happened or not, it characterized the British Redcoats as nonreligious. In a very religious community, this story portrayed the enemy as somehow un-Godlike. This characterization is often important in times of war, where one side views the other as "not fully human." It seems to make the battle and reasons for killing another person more justified.

In another story, Mrs. Elizabeth (Hinche) Wright (Amos Wright's first wife), with quick thinking and forethought, hid the church's communion silver in a new soap barrel in the tavern, thus saving these precious treasures from possible British confiscation.[67] An alternative story has the communion silver placed in the soap barrels by Susannah Robinson, a woman who lived in a white house next door to the meetinghouse (which has now been torn down). She is said to have taken the communion plate home and hid it in her softsoap barrel, in an arch under the chimney, until the Redcoats left Concord. This story reflected some of the cleverness of townspeople to the British occupation. This communion silver now resides and is on display at the Concord Museum. First Parish uses these original silver pieces for certain ceremonial events.

When the Redcoats entered the Wright Tavern's taproom, Mrs. Daniel Taylor (Lydia) noticed four musket balls laying out, and in the confusion, she quickly hid them in her apron. The Regulars then sat and ate breakfast. When it came time to pay the bill, she thought she was handing them change, but instead, she gave them the musket balls. When an officer asked what she wanted him to do with the balls, she said, "Sir, I would use them in a Firelock if I had one."

Soon after the Redcoats entered the town, Phebe Emerson, wife of William Emerson, learned of this event from their enslaved Black man, Frank Benson. It is told that he rushed into her room with an axe, saying, "The Redcoats have come!" She fainted but quickly revived. She then saw to the needs of her guests, a small group of women and children who took refuge in her home, the "Old Manse." She felt hurt that Reverend Emerson didn't remain with her and felt she needed him more than the militia troops did. From the location of her home, they were able to watch the events happening at the North Bridge.[68]

In another incident, Ephraim Jones, the son of the man who built the Wright Tavern, was an innkeeper of the Jones Tavern in Concord. The tavern serviced the county jail that Jones oversaw as an appointee of the Middlesex County court. He was defiant against the British and locked all the doors to the jail and his inn. When the grenadiers attempted to open it, he refused. They summoned Major Pitcairn to address the issue. Because the inn and jail were not considered private property, Pitcairn ordered Jones, at gunpoint, to open them. Jones soon complied. Pitcairn also knew that cannons were buried nearby and demanded that Jones lead him to them. After some resistance, Jones complied, and they discovered three twenty-four-pound cannons buried near the jail. Pitcairn ordered his men to tear them apart and make them useless. He also discovered two people in the jail managed by Jones who had been arrested only a few days before for being Tories and making remarks loyal to the Crown. Pitcairn had them released.[69]

Also in the jail was a Black freeman named Thomas Nichols. He had been arrested in Natick and sent to the jail in Concord. He was charged with inciting a slave rebellion, "enticing divers Servants [slaves] to desert the Service of their Masters." But there was little evidence to support this charge, and he was eventually released. He must have witnessed the destruction of the cannons and the white men released by Major Pitcairn.[70]

Another story occurred in the Jones Inn. As the British Redcoats approached one room, a young servant girl named Hannah Barnes stood in the doorway and would not let the Redcoats enter the room. She said that this was her room, and they could not enter. Imagine the courage of this young woman facing down two or three fully armed soldiers towering over her. They saw a large trunk in the room and asked what was in it. She told them it was hers and they could not search it. The Regulars tried, but she was defiant and told them to go away. Reluctantly, the soldiers moved on.[71]

This was, in fact, not her room and not her trunk. The room evidently had been occupied by Henry Gardner, the treasurer of the Provincial Congress. In the trunk were stored many of the Provincial Congress's papers. This young servant woman protected what would have been a major find by the Redcoats and perhaps could have changed the course of the Provincial Congress. We will never know what would have happened if the Regulars had gotten the names and tax payment records made to Congress instead of the British. Imagine what might have happened if the British had discovered the papers, documents and potential cash of the Provincial Congress. This scenario did not happen because of Hannah Barnes's courage.[72]

When the Regulars entered the home of Joseph Hosmer near the South Bridge, they were met by Lucy Barnes Hosmer. The Regulars were interested in a room where the door was closed. She insisted the Regulars let her mother sleep, and after a brief conversation, they moved on. They did not discover a large supply of muskets, ammunition, musket balls and powder hidden under the large feather mattress on which Hosmer's elderly mother slept. Lieutenant Hosmer was at the North Bridge, serving as the adjutant for the militias.[73]

At Amos Wood's home near the South Bridge, the grenadiers started searching the home for military supplies. Again, Wood was with the other members of the militia. The ladies, including Lydia Wood, living in the home, told the officers that there was one room they were forbidden to enter because an indisposed lady occupied it. The officer told his men to pass by, albeit reluctantly. In this room was a large amount of military supplies, including muskets, munitions and other supplies, but not an "indisposed lady." As they left, the British officers gave each woman a guinea in payment for any trouble they caused.

In addition to munitions, the Redcoats were looking for stockpiles of rations—meat and meal—to feed the Massachusetts army. At the establishment of miller Timothy Wheeler, a locked barn held numerous barrels of flour. The Regulars demanded entry. With no option but to obey, Wheeler escorted the Regulars into the storehouse, only to insist that the barrels belonged to him: "Gentlemen, I am a miller and declare to you that every gill of this is mine." Given their vow to protect private property, the Regulars felt obliged to withdraw. They left behind a vast supply of cornmeal to furnish Johnny cakes for provincial troops. Only a few barrels of flour were Wheeler's own supply.[74]

During one of their searches directed by their map, the British entered Ebenezer Hubbard's flour mill house. There, they found several barrels of flour supposedly for feeding the rebel army. The grenadiers broke open several barrels and rolled them out onto the road. They busted up the barrels, and the flour poured out onto the street, turning it white. It is said the road looked like it had just snowed.[75]

Near the center of town was the Mill Pond, which served the interests of the British, or so they thought. When Regulars found a few barrels of flour and munitions like musket bullets and gunpowder, they just tossed them into the Mill Pond. However, the outer parts of the flour barrels formed a crust that protected most of the flour in the barrels. After the Regulars left Concord, the townspeople merely went into the pond, recovered the munitions and flour, and resupplied their stores.

The British forces searched Colonel Barrett's home and grounds and found none of the supplies said to be stored there. The inhabitants had anticipated their arrival and removed the military stores to the fields and neighboring farms. The fields looked freshly plowed, but the rebels had carefully hidden many of their muskets and supplies within the rows of the field.

As the British searched the grounds, the officers demanded that Rebeckah Barrett serve them breakfast. Summoning her courage, the mistress of the household refused. So, the officers tossed money into her lap. Reluctantly, she responded by saying, "We are commanded to feed our enemies." Later, she said, "This is the price of blood," and she put the money in her pocket.[76]

As discussed earlier, when the British Redcoats entered a community and saw a Liberty Pole, they cut it down to destroy the symbol of the Patriots. They added it to the wood pile they were creating from confiscated supplies. Through their searches that morning, they came upon tools and a few wooden parts for guns. They tossed them into a large wood pile in the center of town. The fire they set caught the nearby courthouse on fire (visible from the Wright Tavern). Martha Moulton, an aged widow and housekeeper for schoolmaster Timothy Minot, pleaded with the British troops to help the townspeople extinguish the flames, but her pleas were ignored. The old woman kept up her appeals until the soldiers finally joined with the townspeople to put out the fire.[77]

As an interesting twist of fate, the smoke from the blaze rose into the sky, where it was detected by militia forces occupying the hill overlooking the North Bridge. Lieutenant Joseph Hosmer started pointing out smoke billowing above the trees and questioned, "Will you let them burn the town down?"[78] The militiamen started to believe that the British were burning the town to the ground. Although this was not the case, their anger grew more intense and, in many ways, set the conditions for the battle that was soon to follow. As one could imagine, seeing smoke rising from the town center over the trees further strengthened the anger and resolve of the colonial militia. But what was actually happening was quite different. This was a rare case of cooperation between the Redcoat Regulars and the townspeople in successfully putting out the fire.

At the North Bridge, things were starting to heat up. As more militia arrived from the surrounding towns of Acton, Sudbury and Littleton, the colonial force grew larger. The British Redcoats were becoming outnumbered. British captain Walter Laurie commanded about 115 men. The provincials on the other side of the river numbered about 400. Laurie sent an urgent message to Colonel Smith seeking reinforcements. The two sides waited and watched each other across about eight hundred yards of open land and the bridge. The wait was tedious and tense. Colonel Barrett held a brief counsel with the other militia commanders. They did not want to start the war, but they were witnessing smoke arising from the town center and worried that it was being burned by the British forces there. After the conference with his officers, Colonel Barrett walked in front of his men and told them to load their guns.[79]

On Colonel Barrett's order, the militia started to march to broaden their line in order to demonstrate their strength and numbers. The sheer number of militia soldiers and their military discipline impressed and scared the British Regulars. There were now over 450 militia soldiers emerging at them from the hill. These were no mere "country folk," as the Regulars were led to believe; many were seasoned fighters. Several British Regulars started tearing up planks in the bridge but stopped when they saw the militia force moving toward them. The militia continued marching slowly toward the bridge. The British backed across the bridge and tried to get into their "street formation," a series of lines where the Regulars on the first line would fire and then return to the back and reload while the next line would move forward and fire. This was all precision movement for traditional military battles. But here, things were different. The British force couldn't get their formation in order, and the militias kept approaching the bridge and some started to cross it.[80]

In response, the British fired a series of warning shots over the heads of the colonial militias. Then, just as suddenly, the British took direct aim and fired. Captain Laurie lost control of his men at that time. Several colonial soldiers were killed instantly, including Isaac Davis, the commander of the Acton militia, and his younger officer Abner Hosmer. At that instant, Major Buttrick leaped into the air and said, "Fire, fellow soldiers, for God's sake, fire!" There were cries of "Fire, fire, fire!" and so began the battle and the Revolutionary War.[81]

The battle lasted only a few minutes. Two Minutemen (both from Acton) were killed and four were wounded; for the British, three Regulars were killed and nine were wounded.[82] White smoke filled the air. It was hard to see the enemy on either side, and shots rang out in wild succession. More colonial militias started moving toward the bridge, and the Redcoats retreated and ran back toward Concord. They left their dead and wounded soldiers behind. The reinforcements from Concord had been delayed and never arrived in time.

The Battle of Concord was over, but its reverberations would continue. While the battle in Lexington caused the death of eight Americans (and no British), this battle in Concord was the first one where a militia officer ordered his men to fire upon British forces. It took several months before the impact of this battle would shape the rise of independence among the other American colonies. It took sixty-two years before Ralph Waldo Emerson, grandson of Reverend Emerson, said in the "Concord Hymn" (1837) that this would now be referred to as "the shot heard round the world."[83]

Back in Concord village, the report of things not going well at the North Bridge must have been surprising and devastating to Colonel Smith and Major Pitcairn. Colonel Smith led a small force of his grenadiers to reinforce the infantry at the North Bridge, but the effort was delayed, and they never reached the bridge. When they were within a few hundred yards of the bridge, they came upon Captain Laurie's troops running in fear and confusion from the battle they had just encountered. Several men were injured, and several lay dead. Rather than engaging the colonists, who clearly outnumbered them, Smith decided to retreat to Concord.[84] The militia let them return to Concord without pursuing or firing at them.

The British, too, had their anxiety and fear grow when the story was told of a British soldier who was axed and scalped by a Minuteman; this was not true. As the actual situation evolved, a young British soldier was wounded and left by the retreating Regulars. While he lay seriously wounded, a young (twenty-year-old) Concord militiaman named Ammi White approached him. He was excited by the opportunity to kill a Redcoat, and so almost without thinking, he pulled out his hatchet and swiftly stuck the grenadine in the forehead. The soldier fell back to the ground, and while he was still barely alive, White hit him two more times in the head with his hatchet, killing him. White then ran off toward his farm. There was one report that actually the grenadine was in severe pain and White put him out of his misery.[85]

When Major Parson's men were returning from Barrett's farm, they crossed the North Bridge and saw the remains of the battle. They also saw the British grenadier who had just been killed less than an hour before. They reported to other grenadiers that their fellow soldier had been scalped, with his ears hacked off. This fed more rage and anxiety among the British Regulars, who now strongly wanted to return to Boston. The rumor spread like wildfire to other Regulars when the British finally returned to Boston.[86] Each side created stories to portray their victory or victimization.

Rather than rapidly retreating to Boston, Smith decided to tend to his wounded and allow his men to finish their mission. These events clearly shook him. He assembled his men into formation, disbanded them and reassembled them with no explicit purpose. He marched them in one direction and then another, creating more confusion and concern among the soldiers about his leadership. He was beginning to realize that the twenty-mile march back to Boston might be a perilous one. He would soon find this correct. As he delayed taking action, more and more colonial militias began coming toward Concord and along the road back to Boston.[87] The Bay Road to Lexington and beyond was filled with militia ready for a fight and hearing exaggerated stories from the events in Lexington and Concord.

In the wake of the British withdrawal, townspeople counted their losses. Reuben Brown, a saddler who had served as a courier and scout, suffered the theft of saddles, stirrups, cartridge holders and bridles from his shop by the Redcoats. The British also burned his harness shop when they were leaving Concord. Fortunately, many townspeople extinguished the fire. Mrs. Ezekiel Brown reported that the Redcoats stole various items from her store, including a cotton shirt, a pair of shoes, pewter plates, a pewter basin and silver buttons. But thanks to the quick action and wit of many Concord women, most of the military militia stores were saved from destruction or confiscation.[88]

At about noon, the first British columns began marching back on Bay Road to Lexington and to safety in Boston. The long column marched without drum and fife or customary precision. Horse-drawn chaises were stolen from nearby stables and used to carry the wounded. Knowing that further trouble may await them, a large party was ordered to secure the ridge and protect the flanks of the retreating army. Others were sent out to the low-lying meadows to prepare the road for the main party. This worked for a while. No further fighting occurred for the first mile from Concord.

When the Regulars reached Meriam's Corner, about one mile from Concord Center, shots started to ring out. At first, the British returned fire above the heads of the colonists. These were warning shots to stay back. But the colonists were not so kind and aimed with accuracy and deadly precision. More British Regulars started being shot, killed and left behind by the British as they tried to advance away from the attacking forces.[89] Robert Gross in *Minutemen and Their World*, George Tolman in *Wright's Tavern* and David Hackett Fischer in *Paul Revere's Ride* all describe the British retreat from Concord and what they faced on their return to Boston.

In Concord, one can imagine that many of the women, children and returning Minutemen in the town crowded into the Wright Tavern and perhaps other taverns with both jubilation and concern. This was the first major battle between the colonial militias and the British Regulars. Would this mean that war would start, or would this be seen as another troubling event (like the Boston Massacre) between the Regulars and Patriots? Would General Gage send more troops to Concord to punish the citizens for their rebellion? No one knew what this day would mean and what the consequences would be to their town and to the emerging struggle for independence. But what occurred after the British left Concord was more devastating and destructive to the British forces than what occurred at the North Bridge. As more and more militias started arriving from surrounding towns on the road between Concord and Lexington and Menotomy (now Arlington), the British came under intense fire. As they ran, they often fell into more traps of fresh militia Minutemen. Fischer, in *Paul Revere's Ride*, describes how this retreat from Concord to Lexington "shattered" the British Regulars.[90]

In total, the British encountered significantly greater losses than the colonists. According to Fischer, over 3,900 colonial militias were involved in the battles and 1,500 British Regulars. On the road back to Boston, the colonists lost 50 soldiers, 39 wounded and 5 reported missing. The British lost 73 soldiers, 174 injured and 25 reported missing. This reflects that 2.4 percent of the Minuteman militias and 18 percent of the British forces were killed, injured or missing. It was an overwhelming defeat for the British and the beginning of what would become known as the Revolutionary War or the War for Independence. It would soon spread to Boston and other colonies.

Soon after the battles in Concord and Lexington, Amos Doolittle, an engraver, and Ralph Earle, a Connecticut painter, came to Concord to paint and publish four scenes from that day. They based their depictions of the events on eyewitness accounts by the citizens. They are believed to be highly accurate accounts of what British soldiers and citizens faced that day.[91] The engravings show the Wright Tavern in the center with over seven hundred British Redcoats marching past.

These actions must have changed the mindset about whether the colonists were protesting or rebelling against the limitations placed on their rights. Although the consequences of these actions were highly uncertain, this day

The British Expeditionary Force arriving in Concord on April 19, 1775. *Engraving by Amos Doolittle, New York Public Library Digital Collections.*

ultimately signaled the beginning of the American Revolution. The battle in Lexington, the British defeat in Concord and the slaughter of British Regular soldiers on Bay Road demonstrated that these colonists were going to fight for their independence. No one knew where this would lead or whether the actions of the Provincial Congress would last. There was no Declaration of Independence or establishment of a new country yet. Many other colonies and the British government in London did not know for several months the extent of what happened on this day. But on this day, these people took their stand and successfully challenged the strongest military force in the world. The primary mission of these colonists was to protect and regain their rights. Still, something important happened that perhaps changed their mindset and that of many others in the American colonies. The people in Concord resisted and deceived the British Regulars when they attempted to search their homes. Women and men alike stood up to this major pressure. Their message went out quickly to other American colonies and the British Crown. Something important had changed, and the Wright Tavern was at the center of these events.

In his book *An Historic Tour*, John J. Busch provides a poem about the events in Concord on that day:[92]

The legend tells that in this house
The silver of the church
Was hidden in a keg of soap
Away from British search,
Certain it is her ancient creed
So guarded sacred things,
That to her solemn verities
No "soft soap" ever clings.

One Brown once kept the Tavern Wright,
And a brave man was he,
For in the Boston Tea Party,
he helped to pour the tea.
This fact is chiseled on his stone, and
grave stones never lie,
But always speak of living truth just as
Do you and I.

Chapter 7

WRIGHT TAVERN ENTERS A NEW ERA

Amos Wright was a quiet, gentle, retiring man, so the events of April 19 must have tested his patience. We can be sure that for days following, the tavern became a center for discussions and gossip, which likely depleted what liquid refreshments remained in the tavern after the British had left. While Concord would not see additional battles in the impending war, the events of this day surely set a new course for the future of these people. The citizens remained actively engaged in the war effort. It changed the thinking of many who tried to remain neutral and hardened the resolve of both the Loyalists and Patriots.[93] In decades later, people came to Concord to see the North Bridge and the Wright Tavern and learn the stories of what happened in Concord at the beginning of the American Revolution.

In Massachusetts, military mobilization intensified on both the British and provincial sides. Occupied Boston became an armed camp, as Patriots fled into the countryside and Loyalists found sanctuary in the capital. In Cambridge, George Washington oversaw his fledgling Continental army, whose soldiers obtained barracks at Harvard College and whose students and faculty, in turn, found a welcome in Concord. With the encouragement of Reverend William Emerson (Harvard class of 1761), 143 students and faculty secured quarters in Concord homes and pursued their studies in the village meetinghouses and public buildings around the town. For all the liveliness they brought to the town, the students didn't particularly enjoy "country life." So, soon after British forces evacuated from Massachusetts in March 1776, Harvard quickly reclaimed its space. The intense debates and raucous parties of the students were heard in Wright Tavern no more.[94]

A year after the Battle of Concord, in December 1775, Daniel Taylor sold the Wright Tavern—land, building and all the contents—to Samuel Swan of Charlestown, a wig-maker familiar with upper-class tastes. Swan was one of many Charlestown residents seeking refuge in the countryside after his home was burned by British Regulars during the Battle of Bunker Hill.[95] Under Swan's management, the alehouse was initially very successful in supplying food and drink to the many civilian and army officers in and out of the town to oversee the provision of military stores to the Continental forces. Swan renovated and expanded the building to provide a long dining room for guests. Then, things began to change. The outlay was perhaps not well timed. By the time Swan finished the renovations, the selectmen and other municipal officers had moved their meetings to the rival alehouse on the Bay Road. Perhaps for this reason, Swan welcomed other businesses into his space. The basement became a bakery run by the Kettell brothers (William, John and Thomas), Swan's nephews and fellow refugees from Charlestown. Swan oversaw the tavern above.[96]

During and following the Revolutionary War, the economic conditions in Concord and throughout much of Massachusetts were very challenging. The war effort utilized many men who would normally be tending the fields, stores and shops. Food supplies and animal stock were often sent to support the war effort. Inflation was high, and the yields of the fields were declining because of over-farming over the years. It was difficult to retain the children of the town and provide good income opportunities or new farmland. Many of the young adults sought larger towns to find employment or headed west to find new lands for farming. The war efforts created many uncertainties for the townspeople.[97] But by the late 1790, the fortunes of the town had begun to turn around as small shops began and trade expanded for the Americans and Concord farmers and tradespeople. Concord again became a center of economic activity.[98]

In 1798, the Middlesex Hotel opened on the corner opposite the Wright Tavern. It was built by John Richardson after he opened a tavern in what is now the Catholic rectory and exchanged that property for the location of what would soon become known as the Middlesex Hotel. It provided food, drink, a large ballroom and private meeting rooms. People began frequenting the new hotel.[99] Consequently, the Wright Tavern's business declined dramatically. Where it was once a thriving center of Concord life, the tavern saw fewer visitors. The Wright Tavern lost much of its appeal and center of importance in Concord town life. It was viewed as an old building that lacked the space and amenities of newer locations.

The Middlesex Hotel continued to operate for several years under a series of hotelkeepers hired by Richardson. He sold it to Thomas D. Wesson and Gershom Fay in 1825. Wason acquired Fay's interests after a few years. The hotel was very popular until about 1845, when it burned down. Colonel John Wilson was the manager at the time. It was rebuilt the next year but was facing struggles with the growing temperance community in Concord. With the installation of the new railroad in the mid-1840s and the movement of the courthouse to Lowell, business at the hotel declined steadily. With fewer people traveling by wagon and needing food, drink and lodging, the hotel ceased operations in 1882. After standing vacant for several years, it was torn down in 1900.[100]

With the surrender of the British in Yorktown and the signing of the Treaty of Paris on September 3, 1783, the Revolutionary War ended, and the formation of the United States began. As the country was forming, all did not progress smoothly. In Massachusetts, as well as several other colonies, the vision of a free and fair country was unfilled for thousands of people. These men and some women who served in the Continental army were largely unpaid or not reimbursed for the heavy expenses they invested in the War for Independence. The country itself was mired in severe economic conditions, and there was little currency with which to buy goods and services. The taxes were more than what had been imposed by the British. The new government, especially in Massachusetts, arrested several debtors and seized their farms and homes for nonpayment of taxes. This was particularly difficult in Western Massachusetts. The Massachusetts government refused to hear their complaints and continued to impose new taxes and harsh penalties.

On August 29, 1786, over 500 militiamen stormed the county seat in Northampton. Officials blocked the court and prevented them from seizing more property. Similar protests began happening in other communities, including Concord. The "Regulators," as they called themselves, were attempting to regulate the operation of the courts. The local authorities were unable to mobilize the militia to keep open the courts; in fact, many of the rank and file joined the protest movement. By early 1787, the Massachusetts governor, James Bowdoin, sought to quell the insurrection by raising an army of 1,200 men, which grew to 4,000 under the command of General Benjamin Lincoln, using funds supplied by local merchants. Lincoln had also served as secretary of the First Massachusetts Provincial Congress in

Concord in 1774. In Concord, Roger Brown, a clothier who lived in the western section of town, raised a unit to serve under Lincoln. Tensions intensified in the Bay State, especially in Concord, where the courthouse near the Wright Tavern was closed because of these desperate rebels.

A reluctant and unassuming Daniel Shays, a farmer from Pelham, Massachusetts, and a veteran of Bunker Hill and many significant battles of the Revolutionary War, became involved and ultimately assumed leadership of the insurgency.[101] He ended up leading a group of six hundred men in September 1786. They shut down the courts in Springfield by using their force but without using violence. The protest alarmed leading figures throughout the new nation. Henry Knox, a commander during the Revolutionary War and the first U.S. secretary of war, kept George Washington up to date.

On January 25, 1787, the rebellion came to a head. On a deep, snow-covered morning, approximately 1,200 men under the command of Shays approached the federal arsenal in Springfield. They were seeking to acquire additional arms and munitions to support their protests. Many men had guns, but others wielded clubs and pitchforks. Another 1,000 men were on their way to join Shays in what was declared a "rebellion" by Governor Bowdoin.

As Shays's men approached the arsenal, the defenders fired shots over their heads. Then, the army took deadly aim, killing four and wounding over twenty. The farmers and veterans fled immediately. A week later, Lincoln's men ambushed Shays and his men and swiftly crushed the rebellion. Shays and many of his leaders fled north to Vermont, gaining refuge in what was an independent republic at the time.

The short-lived rebellion changed this emerging country. First, it demonstrated major problems with the Articles of Confederation. There came calls for a stronger national government, and it influenced the debate in drafting the new U.S. Constitution in the summer of 1787. Second, people felt the state government had been too harsh and sought to address the treatment of these men. Under a new governor, John Hancock, the state reduced taxes, passed a moratorium on debt collections and pardoned Shays and his fellow rebels. The Concord courthouse opened and returned to trying crimes, probating estates and other normal business.[102]

On March 9, 1793, Samuel Swan sold the tavern property because it was no longer financially sustainable and returned to Charlestown. The new owner, Captain Reuben Brown, was a successful saddler whose business at the entrance to the village on Lexington Road provided the resources to sustain the tavern.[103] His ownership was short-lived. In December 1793, only nine months after his purchase, he transferred the inn to the partnership of Francis Jarvis and Thomas Safford. Under the new owners, the building was turned into a bakery. It would supply fresh and delicious baked goods to the townspeople longer than it ever served drinks to that point.

Francis Jarvis became a very important member of the Concord community. He was born in Dorchester, Massachusetts, in 1768 and was the son of John and Elizabeth Jarvis. About the time of his father's death, Francis went to live with John Richardson, a baker in Watertown. There, he learned the trade and became an excellent baker. John Richardson, who was discussed earlier, moved to Concord in 1778 and took over an old tavern across the street from the Wright Tavern and then ultimately built what became the Middlesex Hotel. Jarvis, at age twenty-one, joined him as an apprentice in 1789. Here, he tended the bar and supervised some of the operations. In 1790, he partnered with Thomas Safford to expand the bakery business from this location. In 1793, Jarvis and Safford bought the Wright Tavern from Brown and moved the bakery into the tavern.[104]

Jarvis and Safford used the kitchen built for the Kettells when Swan owned the building. There is a note in the Groundroot Preservation's Historic Structures Report and the Cole Report that a beam in the attic has Jarvis's name or initials and the date "1787," five years before he bought the building. This indicates that he may have spent a lot of time in the building before buying it from Brown.

Francis Jarvis married Millicent Hosmer, daughter of Nathan Hosmer, in October 1793 in a ceremony officiated by Reverend Ezra Ripley. They lived in the Wright Tavern and had seven children. His relationship with Safford did not last long; in 1795, Jarvis bought out Stafford, who moved on to Lancaster. Jarvis evidently made major changes to the building to accommodate his large family and thriving bakery. His modifications may have included removing one of the central chimneys and replacing it with five fireplaces in the Federalist style (two on the main floor, two on the second floor and one in the basement). This type of fireplace was very fashionable at the time. The records are unclear whether these changes were made by Samual Swan when he extended the Ell beyond the original construction in the 1780s or by Jarvis in the early 1800s.[105]

Jarvis joined the Social Circle Club in 1798 and engaged with other members of the Concord community to discuss politics, town affairs and a wide range of topics. The Social Circle was formed in 1794 and lasted as an important influence on community life until 1882. Its membership was limited to men of means, and only twenty-five members were allowed at a

Left: Francis Jarvis, baker at the Wright Tavern, circa 1820. *Permission granted from the Corinthian Lodge of Concord, Massachusetts.*

Right: A portrait of Reverend Ezra Ripley. *Permission granted by First Parish in Concord, 2023.*

time. They met on Tuesday evenings from October to March in a member's home to discuss common issues of the day. Few issues were presented or discussed at the town meeting without first being deliberated by the Social Circle. They operated outside of public view, but they focused on matters of the public good. Consensus was relatively easy because not only were the members of a similar social class in the town, but they also built considerable trust in each other over the years of meetings and discussions. It was a badge of honor to belong, and Francis Jarvis was a very active member until his death. When someone in the group died, often another member would write a memoir of the individual. Edward Jarvis, the third son of Francis and himself a member of the Social Circle, wrote a memoir for his father. It is unknown whether the Social Circle ever met in the Wright Tavern, but it is likely since Francis Jarvis was an early member.

Francis Jarvis continued the baking business until 1805, when his health deteriorated. To ease the burden of the bakery business, he opened a variety store with a new partner, Charles Hammond, son-in-law of Reuben Brown. This prospered for only two years before Hammond moved to Maine. With Hammond gone, Jarvis resumed the bakery and recruited his namesake,

Hand drawing of Wright Tavern, circa 1800. Francis Jarvis was a baker and owner of the building at that time.

Francis Jr., as a partner. Francis Jarvis & Sons became an important stop along the wagon route to and from Boston and beyond as a purveyor of refreshments when Middlesex Court was in session, the militia practiced and drilled on the common and town meetings were held. The bakery gained fame for its rolls, pies and doughnuts.

Francis Jarvis became a deacon at First Parish in 1812. He was also, during much of this time, in charge of the funds of First Parish. He was rigorous about the accuracy of accounting for every penny of the church's activities. The debts and credits were rigorously balanced each month. He had only three months of formal education when he was a child, but his constitution and tenacity enabled him to be very successful. He was an eager learner. Though he had little education, he was an avid reader and lover of books. He encouraged young men eager to learn and loaned them books from an extensive library he had accumulated over the years. The deacon also had easy access to the collection of the Concord Charitable Library Society, which was housed in a room of the former tavern. In 1792, early in his career, he considered abandoning his bakery and attending Harvard College, but Safford talked him out of it. It is said that he regretted this decision, but he stayed by the oven. His son Edward would inherit this love of books.

The early 1800s were a time of growing prosperity and development in Concord, especially when the Middlesex Court was in session. Court Week was a regular holiday. People set up stalls on the common to sell a host of goods. Rum, brandy, gin, beer, wine and toddies were available at the stores. Other stores retailed farm commodities, baked goods and seasonal produce. Horse trading went on, as did races—and gambling on the winners and losers. The extravaganza was a good excuse for children to skip school. It made for good business at Francis Jarvis's bakery.[106]

For most of Jarvis's life, he rarely ate meat. He did not drink alcohol or spirits, though he was generous in following custom and giving spirits to men who worked for him. He took great interest in town affairs but rarely served in a political post except for a brief period representing Concord as a Federalist in the state legislature. He took great interest in rebuilding the town's poorhouses and supported the schools. In his mind, education was the way out of poverty.

In 1824, President James Monroe extended an invitation to the Marquis de Lafayette of France to come to America and honor those who fought for and supported the War for Independence. Monroe was the last founding father to be president of the United States. France's role was critical to George Washington and the American forces in the defeat of the British. Without their aid, it is unlikely the Continental army would have prevailed. President Monroe wanted to express to Lafayette the gratitude of the nation. President Monroe believed that Lafayette had a profound impact on the early development of the United States. Lafayette's tour took him to twenty-four states over thirteen months (August 1824–September 1825).

On September 2, 1824, the Marquis de Lafayette came to Concord on his way from Boston to New York and ultimately to Mount Vernon. After starting his tour in New Jersey and New York, Lafayette came to Boston. A delegation from Concord came to Boston to meet Lafayette and show him what was regarded as the musket that supposedly fired the first shot. They invited him to come to Concord. Six days later, Lafayette followed the route traveled by the British Regulars on his triumphal trip. The town's leaders hastily organized the parade, reception and welcoming event for Lafayette.

As reported in the *Concord Gazette*, a cavalcade of nearly forty people received Lafayette at the Lexington town line and marched with him to the center of town in front of First Parish and the Wright Tavern. Reverend Ezra Ripley, the longest-serving minister at First Parish, opened with a worship service. It was a hero's welcome.[107]

As Lafayette entered the town, the roar from twenty-four cannons filled the air. Church bells rang out as well. When he reached the field in front of the Wright Tavern and First Parish Church, where tables and chairs had been set up, a sign read, "In 1775, the people of Concord met the enemies of liberty; In 1824, they welcome the bold Assertor of the rights of man— Lafayette." Here, the general was greeted and received by the selectmen of the town and heard remarks from Samuel Hoar Jr. Hoar's remarks ignited a controversy that still persists over whether Concord or Lexington deserves to be known as the starting point of the American Revolution. Hoar claimed the credit and said that Concord was the "first site of forceful resistance."[108] It was a day to celebrate patriotism and the founding of the country. The town's leaders and upper class created the celebration with a large tent in front of the Wright Tavern and First Parish meetinghouse. It was an exclusive event where most of the townspeople could receive glimpses of Lafayette only from a distance.[109]

Refreshments were laid out over the tables, including Jarvis's rolls. Lafayette walked over to meet his old companions in arms, and he spoke easily with the women gathered. The local troops marched in front of him and paid a military salute. He inquired about where the first shot was made, but he was never taken to the North Bridge. When the festivities were completed, the cavalcade marched with Lafayette to the Stow town line on his way to spend the night in Bolton. From there, Lafayette would continue his celebratory journey.[110]

Jarvis's bakery goods were one of the foods at Lafayette's celebration, but it would be one of the last such events for the baker. Jarvis gave the Wright Tavern building to his son Stephen Jarvis for a token one dollar in 1839. Because of his declining health, he moved to live with his other son, Francis, on Colonel John Buttrick's farm. In October 1840, Jarvis finally succumbed to his many ailments and died at age seventy-two. Though he left no will, he had disposed of his property through deeds and bills of sale to his children before his death. He died peacefully during an afternoon nap.[111]

Stephen Jarvis was living in New Orleans and working as a druggist when he acquired the tavern. The building yielded a regular income. Silas Burgess kept a livery stable there, only to be followed in that business by

A very early photograph of the Wright Tavern; the estimated year is 1850.

James M. Billings; his wife, Jerusha; and three children. In 1853, Stephen Jarvis tired of being an absentee landlord and sold the property to Billings, who financed the purchase with a mortgage from the Middlesex Institution for Savings. Though it no longer served drinks, the former Wright Tavern was still profiting on Concord's role as a hub of transportation and trade.[112]

The Wright Tavern was moving on to another chapter in the life of this historic building.

Chapter 8

CONCORD: HOME OF
THE SECOND REVOLUTION

By the half-century point (1850), Concord had grown from 1,500 to about 2,250 citizens. Slavery was prohibited in Massachusetts in 1783. Concord had now become very prosperous, and it was expanding socially, economically and intellectually. Farming was improving, and businesses were growing. Tourists came to visit Concord to see where the Battle of Concord took place and the sights of the town, including the Wright Tavern. At the beginning of the Revolution, the people of Concord did not initially seek to create an independent country, but they wanted to recapture rights that were being taken away. What evolved, however, was a great change. Gross, in *The Transcendentalists and Their World*, indicates that "the age of progress had begun." Social and intellectual thought eventually led to the emergence of Ralph Waldo Emerson, Henry David Thoreau, Louisa May Alcott, Nathaniel Hawthorne and several others a few decades later. Gross refers to this as the "Second Revolution."[113]

By the mid- and late 1800s, Concord had become a center of great intellectual and literary influence. Emerson and Alcott were becoming world-renowned. Transcendentalism emerged as a revolutionary philosophy that offered the perspective that life doesn't center on religious teachings but rather nature and experiencing life and our relationships with the natural world. This philosophy promotes the importance of self-reliance, the infinite potential of each person to do good and the value of experiencing one's emotions and senses. These practices are best found when one immerses oneself in nature. In many ways, this new view of our place in the world built the foundation for today's environmental activism. This philosophy encourages us to consider life's experiences as potential transcendental moments to heighten self-awareness.

Ralph Waldo Emerson became an important thought leader in this movement, as did Bronson Alcott, Margaret Fuller, Nathaniel Hawthorne and many others. Henry David Thoreau became Emerson's protégé and friend and a practitioner of Transcendentalism philosophy. Alcott's School of Philosophy was approximately one-half mile from the Wright Tavern, just near his home. Since these prominent writers lived in Concord, people came here to learn and discuss ideas with them. Imagine the conversations that occurred on the streets, in the living rooms, in taverns and on the walks within the local forests.[114]

Concord was slow to join the developing antislavery movement. When the New England Anti-Slavery Society was founded in 1832, many surrounding towns joined in, but Concord remained reluctant. The residents' reason was more about the concern of the nation with the sudden release of enslaved people versus any support for slavery. The newly formed American Colonization Society (ACS) promoted the gradual reduction in slavery in the future and the return of Black people to their ancestral homes. First Parish, like many other churches in the area, supported the ACS with collection plate contributions. Reverend Ezra Ripley, once a slave owner himself through the marriage of Phebe Emerson, supported this gradual approach to eliminating slavery.[115]

In January 1835, George Thompson, a thirty-one-year-old English abolitionist who was a leading force in the successful efforts to end slavery in Britain, came to speak at First Parish in Concord and the Trinitarian Church. The Middlesex Anti-Slavery Society (founded in 1834) brought Thompson to Concord, and his visit was vilified by the *Concord Gazette*. While the churches were packed, his presentation did not sway many minds. It would take a few more years for the antislavery movement to take hold in Concord.[116]

Additional groups started forming to promote abolition. Mary Merrick Brooks founded the Concord Female Anti-Slavery Society in 1837, which added more pressure and support for antislavery efforts in Massachusetts and the country. John Brown came to Concord on several occasions to solicit funding for his antislavery efforts. Henry David Thoreau and Louisa May Alcott were very active in the antislavery movement. Ralph Waldo Emerson would later become a world-renowned speaker on antislavery and Transcendentalism.

In 1835, Concord celebrated the bicentennial of its founding. A committee was established to plan and organize the activities; it was chaired by John Keyes. The Social Circle was actively engaged in all aspects of the celebration. The town bell ran at precisely 10:30 a.m. to signal the beginning of the festivities, and crowds filled the streets. A parade commenced at the Shepard's Hotel (built in 1824) on Main Street, down past the Middlesex Hotel and then turned right at the Wright Tavern and entered the First Parish meetinghouse. An important element of the parade was the inclusion of the town's children.

All of the children and their parents, except for one, expressed great enthusiasm for their participation. Susan Garrison, one of the few mothers of color, expressed reticence for her twelve-year-old daughter because of an event that she had participated in earlier. Susan was concerned about her ill treatment by white racists in town, and Ellen expressed that "no one would walk with her," to which Abba Maria Prescott rose and said, "I will." This amazed both mothers. Ultimately, Susan agreed, and the two of them, Ellen and Abba Maria, walked hand in hand proudly in the parade despite gazes of curiosity, surprise and admiration.[117]

Ellen Garrison was the daughter of Susan and Jack Garrison and granddaughter of Cesar Robbins, who had been enslaved. Cesar Robbins was one of the many Black men who served in the Revolutionary War. Ellen grew up in postslavery Concord and was a graduate of Concord's public schools. She became an active antislavery advocate. After the Civil War, she went to live in the former Confederate states (Maryland, Virginia and North Carolina) to teach former slaves how to read. She sat with another teacher in the whites-only section of the Baltimore train station waiting room until they were forcibly removed. The manager of the depot was tried for violating the Civil Rights Act of 1866, but the case never reached a verdict. She said of this experience, "I feel as though I ought to strive to maintain my rights.... It will be a stand for others."[118] Later, she moved to Kansas to be a teacher, where she married a farmer and ultimately moved to the antislavery and egalitarian community of Pasadena, California.[119]

Also in 1835, Lemuel Shattuck published his book *History of Concord*. He moved to Concord in 1820 and was fascinated by its history and developing intellectual culture. In this book, he referred to the historic building next to First Parish as the Wright Tavern, named after Amos Wright. The townspeople spoke about Amos Wright and used his name to refer to it for tourists and visitors. The name stuck and has remained for the building regardless of who owned or what operated out of it.[120]

The Woman's Anti-Slavery Society of Concord was founded in 1837. Mary Brooks was one of the founders and served as its president and chief organizer. There are stories that she operated as the "stationmaster" for the Underground Railroad that transported escaped slaves from the South to Canada. It is reported that there were some forty homes in Concord serving as places to hide escaped slaves. This was clearly in violation of federal law, and those found guilty could receive six months in jail and a fine of $1,000 payable to the slave's owner.[121] While there are no records of the Wright Tavern serving as a safe house for runaway slaves, the tavern was clearly a backdrop to the events and the history of these "citizens of Concord."

A few years later, on July 4, 1837, Concord celebrated the completion of the Concord Battle Monument. After several years of discussions and discussion, and gifting of the land by Reverend Ezra Ripley, the monument was completed and ready for dedication. Not much effort was put into the ceremony, and Ralph Waldo Emerson was tasked with writing a hymn for this event. Having just a few weeks to compose the hymn, Waldo Emerson stepped before the gathered crowd. His words captured in a simple but elegant form the spirit that was meant for that day. It was sung by a choir, which included Henry David Thoreau, to the tune of "Old Hundredth." It began:

> *By the rude bridge that arched the flood,*
> *Their flag to April's breeze unfurled,*
> *Here once the embattled farmers stood*
> *And fired the shot heard round the world.*

And ended with:

> *Spirit, that made those heroes dare*
> *To die, and leave their children free,*
> *Bid Time and Nature gently spare*
> *The shaft we raise to them and thee.*

After the song, the people gathered there stood silent for a few moments. For a moment, they all shared a sense of gratitude and patriotism for what had happened there on that day over sixty years before.[122]

Outside the Wright Tavern and on the front lawn of First Parish is a bell. This bell hung in the church for decades and came crashing down during the fire that engulfed the building in 1901. In 1844, Mary Brooks asked Ralph Waldo Emerson to give his first speech against slavery in Concord at

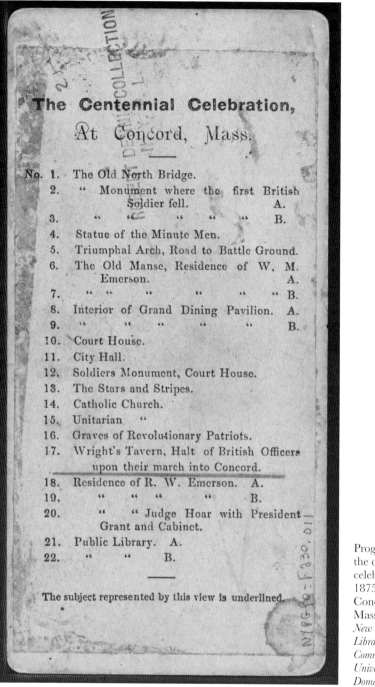

The Centennial Celebration,
At Concord, Mass.

No. 1. The Old North Bridge.
2. " Monument where the first British Soldier fell. A.
3. "   "   "   "   " B.
4. Statue of the Minute Men.
5. Triumphal Arch, Road to Battle Ground.
6. The Old Manse, Residence of W. M. Emerson. A.
7. " " " " " " B.
8. Interior of Grand Dining Pavilion. A.
9. "   "   "   "   " B.
10. Court House.
11. City Hall.
12. Soldiers Monument, Court House.
13. The Stars and Stripes.
14. Catholic Church.
15. Unitarian "
16. Graves of Revolutionary Patriots.
17. Wright's Tavern, Halt of British Officers upon their march into Concord.
18. Residence of R. W. Emerson. A.
19. "   "   "   " B.
20. " " Judge Hoar with President Grant and Cabinet.
21. Public Library. A.
22. "   " B.

The subject represented by this view is underlined.

Program for the centennial celebration, 1875, in Concord, Massachusetts. *New York Public Library, Creative Commons CC0 1.0 Universal Public Domain Dedication.*

the celebration of the emancipation of the slaves in West Indies. Evidently, the sexton refused to ring the bell because he was not authorized to do so. In response, Henry David Thoreau entered the church and rang the bell anyway. He and his family were strongly abolitionists, as were many of the authors and intellectuals of the town.[123]

In 1858, George Prescott acquired the Wright Tavern from an estate settlement at the time of James Billings's death; Samuel Staples served as the assignee of the Billings estate. Little is known about who lived in the building at this time or what happened to Billings's family. Prescott became a military captain, served in the Civil War for the Union and was killed at Gettysburg. Sam Staples was made famous because he was, among other town jobs, the sheriff who arrested Henry David Thoreau for not paying his poll taxes. Thoreau was protesting slavery and the Mexican-American War. Staples did not want to arrest Thoreau and offered to pay his taxes for him, but Thoreau refused and spent one night in the town jail on July 23, 1846. The jail, which no longer stands, was just across the street from the Wright Tavern. Thoreau's experience led him to write and publish *Civil Disobedience*, one of his most famous works.[124] This writing helped shape much of the civil and human rights movements of the twentieth century. It is widely believed that this book inspired Mahatma Gandhi and Dr. Martin Luther King in their approach to nonviolent civil disobedience to fight for people's rights.

President Abraham Lincoln signed the Emancipation Proclamation on January 1, 1863. By his authority as commander-in-chief, Lincoln used this proclamation to free all the slaves in the ten states that were in rebellion with the Union. While many praised this action in Concord and New England, others felt it did not go far enough. Slaves could continue to be held in the Union states. Concord had become a strong antislavery town. Mary Rice was a schoolteacher and active antislavery proponent in the town. In response to Lincoln's limited effort to free all the slaves, in 1864, Mary Rice, together with Mary Peabody Mann (widow of Horace Mann, the noted educator and often referred to as the Father of American Education), wrote a petition and got over 195 Concord children to sign it. Her private school for young children was in the Ell or the extension of the Wright Tavern. The petition asked President Lincoln to free all the slave children in the United States, wherever they lived. This became known as the "Little People's Petition." In his response, Lincoln said that while he truly supported their initiative, he did not have the power to do so.[125] It wasn't until December 18, 1865, with the passage of the Thirteenth Amendment to the U.S. Constitution, that slavery was finally abolished.

"Little People's Petition" sent to Abraham Lincoln, 1864—Library *of Congress*.

This was a time of dramatic changes in Concord, with the rise of antislavery and the movement for women's rights. The country also faced and resolved a rebellion by the southern states and the ending of formal slavery and the American Civil War. Changes in society would continue. And the country, including Concord, expanded economically. By the late 1860s, after the Civil War, the United States economy exceeded that of Great Britain, driven by substantial increases in labor productivity and a growing population primarily due to many immigrants coming to America.[126]

During this time, the Wright Tavern continued to change hands fairly frequently. George Prescott sold his share to Julius M. Smith, a painter, in 1860. Smith (along with Staples) sold the property to Daniel H. Wood in 1864, who then sold the property in 1871 to Lucy L. Brown and George F. Brown. They moved into the building and were recorded as stable keepers, not innkeepers.[127] Concord became full of shops, manufacturing sites and small businesses, including the Wright Tavern. As a result, a strong middle class was growing within this community.

For the next several years, the operators within the building reflected Concord's growth in small businesses. Under the Browns' ownership, the building housed a large array of tenants. Concord supported its own bookstore operated by Captain John Stacy. He was a printer and bookbinder who, in 1846, initially operated a bookstore in the Wright Tavern but soon moved to a more fashionable building on the Milldam.[128]

The building then became occupied by Joe Parks, who operated a tinsmith shop, followed by William Wimms, who sold shoes. Frank Potter and his son Billy were the makers of Potter's Hair Balm, a Macassar oil to give men's hair a smooth and stylish look. Macassar oil is made from various vegetable oils like coconut, palm and Kusum. They operated this business out of the Wright Tavern and were quite successful. It is interesting to note that even though the uses of the building changed hands many times, the name stuck, and for good reason. The businesses constantly turned over; the building endured. In a Special Collection at the Concord Free Public Library is a poster advertising the "Old Wright Tavern" for sale at an auction by R. Vose and Company on May 6, 1875. The property, still in the hands of the Browns, included a "Mansion house containing 22 rooms, a large stable and a carriage house." While a note on the poster indicates the property was sold to Samuel Staples for $7,300, the deed records indicate it was sold to George Brooks in May 1875. Brooks was an attorney in Concord at the time and may have been acting for Samuel Staples.[129]

To further witness innovations in Concord, in 1849, Ephraim Wales Bull developed what was to become known as the Concord grape. Bull experimented for years with different seedlings before finding the right mix to offer some fruit with robust flavor and able to tolerate New England winters. It wasn't until 1854 that this new grape made its debut. Dr. Thomas Welch, a New Jersey dentist, gathered pounds of Concord grapes from trellises in front of his house and cooked the grapes in his kitchen until they became a juice. Welch and his wife squeezed the juice through cloth bags into quarter bottles and stopped them with cork and wax. The process was successful, and it gave rise to a new industry: the production of fruit juices. Creating a grape that was turned into a famous product is another example of the ingenuity that was fostered in mid-nineteenth-century Concord and the United States.[130]

In 1866, Charles L. Heywood built an expansive amusement park on the western side of Walden Pond. This was known as the Walden Lake Grove Excursion Park. It included its own train station from Boston and points west, baseball fields, swings, food concessions, a music pantheon and a dance hall. People could change into their swimming attire on floating bathhouses and rent boats to explore Walden Pond. There was a racetrack for a new invention called the bicycle for the speed adventurer.[131] The park attracted a wide range of citizens from Boston and the surrounding area and helped put Concord on the tourist map. Concord was becoming a bustling community.

In his book *Wright's Tavern*, Tolman reports that Seth Stone operated an unlawful business from the basement of the Wright Tavern. Customers who knew the password and countersign could receive "clandestine beverages." Although it was highly popular, the alcoholic beverage served, according to Tolman, was quite awful.

The Wright Tavern at that time was not well regarded by the town citizens and was viewed as a rundown inn. Brooks hired Otis Penniman, born in Concord in 1867, to manage the Wright Tavern. He had once overseen the town's poorhouse on Walden Street, so why not? He ran the tavern as a hotel, providing rooms for some of the town's poor who labored by day in the village. The town paid the charges. It is possible that the tenants occupied the rooms on the third floor.[132] Amid the changing clientele were two long-term residents: William Ward, who "did nothing in particular," according to Tolman, and John Davis, who had tried and failed to keep his own hotel. Clearly, Brooks was facing the hazards of the hospitality business.

On April 12, 1875, Concord celebrated the centennial of the Battle of Concord and the start of the Revolutionary War. Over twenty thousand visitors were expected to attend. The guests include President Ulysses S. Grant, Vice President Henry Wilson and Massachusetts Governor William Gaston. Other cabinet secretaries and governors of several New England states attended. It was a bitterly cold day, and the ceremony planners built a stage near the Old North Bridge to hold only about one hundred dignitaries. Unfortunately, two hundred individuals considered themselves dignitaries and stepped on the stage. Soon after the opening announcement by Judge Ebenezer Rockwood Hoar and the prayer by Reverend Grindall Reynolds from First Parish, the stage began to sag and then collapse altogether. Everyone was sent tumbling into the mud. When the confusion subsided, the presidential dignitaries moved on to Lexington. Later that night, the citizens of Concord enjoyed a large dance and celebration.

George Brooks sold the Wright Tavern to Judge Ebenezer Hoar and Reuben N. Rice in 1882. It is believed that after attending the centennial celebration, even with its dramatic conclusion, Hoar and Rice were concerned about the future of the declining inn. They had witnessed many other very historic homes and buildings being torn down and replaced by more modern structures. They must have known the historical importance of the Wright Tavern, but they saw the building was not being well maintained and were likely concerned that an unsightly drinking establishment would emerge next to the First Parish Church.

Hoar was born in Concord, served as the U.S. attorney general under President Ulysses S. Grant from 1869 to 1870 and was the first head of the newly formed Department of Justice. In this latter role, he developed what is now the Department of Justice, reporting to the president of the United States. Ebenezer was the son of Samuel Hoar, a graduate of Harvard, a Massachusetts state senator as an antislavery Whig and later a representative in Congress. He was an active member and leader at First Parish in Concord.

Rice was a successful railroad executive in Detroit, Michigan. A failure as a merchant, he rebuilt his fortunes on the railroad. The Fitchburg Railroad was founded in 1842. This train line served a large paper mill in Fitchburg at the time, and the owner, Alvah Crocker, financed much of the railroad. Construction began in 1842 by the Fitchburg Railroad Corporation, and in 1845, the line was officially opened. It was an engineering achievement to address the hills and rivers that lie between Fitchburg and Boston. While Henry David Thoreau objected to the train line being laid near his beloved Walden Pond, there are reports he was quite fascinated by the train and its technology.[133] It is reported that Thoreau bought one of the houses used by the Irish railroad laborers when they were building the rails near Concord and used parts of this shack to build his cabin on the now-famous Walden Pond. He was particularly interested in the vegetation that grew along the tracks, as well as the layers of soil that were visible from the cut of the railroad. He often walked along the rail tracks between Concord Village and Walden Pond.

Over time, the railroad turned Concord into a "suburban community" that put Boston within easy commutable distance. This transformed Concord from primarily an agricultural and farming community to one that supported small industrial businesses and people working in Boston. It retains many of the small businesses and craft stores within its boundaries. The railroad made it much easier to receive and transport their goods to Boston markets and beyond.

By this time, the Wright Tavern was showing its age and becoming an eyesore in Concord Center. In a memoir of his life, Rice states that he spent a lot of money in "fitting up the old Wright Tavern and its surroundings and gave the use of his share to the experiment of a People's Club," which lasted only a year or two. It is reported in the July 8, 1892 edition of the *Concord Enterprise* that "extensive work was done to the tavern."[134] It is likely that the Ell, which had been expanded approximately fifteen feet beyond the original construction by Samual Swan, was removed. The town was expanding Main Street to better intersect with Lexington Road, and the extension had to be removed. Also, the road was raised so that the first level of the tavern was now partially below the grade level of the road.[135] By his will, Rice sold his interest in the Wright Tavern to First Parish for $1,500.

Upon Rice's death in 1885, Judge Hoar sold his interests in the Wright Tavern to First Parish for a token one dollar, the same sum by which Francis Jarvis had transferred title to his son Stephen. He then paid the first year of taxes and stipulated that the income from the tavern be used to pay down any debt incurred by First Parish, which was approved by a vote of the congregation.

Hoar and Rice felt First Parish could sustain and care for this historic building better than their heirs. Their vision and foresight enabled the Wright Tavern to be saved from the progress and building growth occurring in Concord in the late nineteenth century.[136] Although the building has undergone many changes, each adapting to its particular uses needed at the time, it retains much of its original character. We will forever be indebted to Hoar and Rice for their concerns about this historic building and their foresight in preserving it for future generations.

Chapter 9

FIRST PARISH IN CONCORD
BECOMES THE PROPRIETOR

Accoording to the First Parish annual report of 1888, income from the Wright Tavern paid the outstanding debt as well as plumbing and carpentry repairs. The report also stated that First Parish needed to decide what to do with the building. For that purpose, First Parish established the Trustees of Parish Donations to manage the Wright Tavern and other properties owned by the church. The Wright Tavern quickly became an essential feature of First Parish.

Concord shared in the country's growth, prosperity and volatility of an economy increasingly driven by industrialization and monopolies. There was limited taxation or controls on capitalism. The wealthy continued to accumulate huge wealth, while the poor and those with minimal income struggled with everyday survival. Many of the living standards were defined by ethnicity and social class. Often, immigrant boys and girls dropped out of school in their early teens in order to take jobs and help the family meet their financial needs. Small shops met the needs of most town residents, and the rich would travel to Boston or New York for shopping and entertainment. According to Sherblom in *Concord Stories*, "Education and social standing drove wealth, and wealth drove education and social standing."[137]

Soon after taking ownership, First Parish returned the Wright Tavern to an inn with a restaurant and living quarters for guests. Over the next sixty years, it hired a series of innkeepers to operate the building. There is little information about the renters or events that occurred early in the twentieth century. William Rand of Cambridge rented the tavern for $300.00 a year in 1894 and paid $328.50 in 1895. Records show that his occupation was a hotel keeper. Rand rehabilitated the tavern, giving him some notoriety, which enabled him to advance his career elsewhere. When he left in 1899, he was succeeded by Nellie F. Tarleton, who was the twenty-seven-year-old daughter of a hotel keeper. Tarleton, who developed "not always attractive placards and signs," kept the building in good working condition to the satisfaction of her customers.[138]

In 1901, George Tolman, who was the secretary of the Concord Antiquarian Society, wrote a book on the tavern called *Wright's Tavern*. He was born in Concord in 1836 and was the son of Elisha Tolman, a shoemaker and leather dealer in Concord. George attended Concord's public schools and graduated from Harvard College in 1858. He worked for the New England Farms and became involved with the Concord Antiquarian Society, dedicating over forty years of his life to the society. Tolman was critical to organizing and expanding the society's collections and library. He published numerous papers, including ones on the Wright Tavern, before he wrote his book.

First Parish selected John J. Busch to operate the tavern for the next several years. When Busch operated the Wright Tavern, his menu included a fine dinner. While he was in this role, it appears that Busch wrote a book about Concord, *A Historic Tour: A Pilgrimage to the Birthplace of American Liberty and the Homes of Our Foremost Authors*.

In 1910, Charles C. Willman and his wife, Louisa, started renting the building. He was regarded as a "competent hotel man," and the census reported their household had a cleaner, two cooks and a livery driver. They occupied the building for about seven years.

From about 1918 to 1925, Henry Grieme rented the tavern for about twenty dollars per month; this grew to sixty-five dollars per month. Federal census says that Grieme had emigrated from Germany in 1882 and was working with his wife, Teresa, as a cook in a hotel; we presume this was the Wright Tavern. This was during and slightly after the "Great World War" (World War I), which became an era of great prosperity. Following the war, the general mood in Concord and the country at large was festive and active. Concord saw many tourists and enjoyment of the town's many historical sites. The Wright Tavern was marketed with postcards as a place that provides "Food for the Hungry and Rest for the Weary."

In 1924, the Reverend Loren MacDonald, who had been the minister at First Parish for about thirty years, suddenly died within a few hours of contracting food poisoning. His death was caused by a serious mistake.

WRIGHT'S TAVERN.

Postcard of the Wright Tavern, circa 1901. *Courtesy of the Concord Free Public Library.*

According to Peter Mitchell,[139] in those days, people often used arsenic to treat fruit crops for insects. The poison would take a few days to become inert, and then the fruits would be safe to eat. MacDonald had cherry trees in his yard, and a kind neighbor decided to spray them with arsenic as a favor to him. Unfortunately, he forgot to warn MacDonald of this gesture, and later the same day, his wife, Mary Bygrave MacDonald, baked Reverend MacDonald a large cherry pie, his favorite. It is said Reverend MacDonald ate two helpings of this delicious (but dangerous) pie. He died soon after eating the pie.

Reverend MacDonald's death left Mary and three young children without any source of income. There were no pensions then or Social Security, and a minister's salary did not allow for much wealth creation. A group of First Parish parishioners and friends were very concerned about this situation. They learned that Mary had, at one time, run a tearoom, so they asked her if she would like to run the Wright Tavern. She said yes, and so they formed Wright Tavern Incorporated to lease the building and install Mary as the innkeeper. Church records show people pledged between $200 and

THE WRIGHT TAVERN - 1747
CONCORD, MASSACHUSETTS. "FOOD FOR THE HUNGRY, REST FOR THE WEARY."

Postcard of the Wright Tavern. The source is a photograph of the postcard, circa 1930. "Food for the Hungry, Rest for the Weary." *Postcard owned by the Wright Tavern Legacy Trust.*

$1,000 to support this nonprofit entity. It is reported that extensive repairs and improvements were made to the building to accommodate the new innkeeper. A large room was added off the back of the building in 1924/25, as the dining and tearoom for this newly renovated Wright Tavern. Mary operated the building for about ten to twelve years until she and her grown children moved on.[140]

Frank W. Tucker, a resident of Arlington, Massachusetts, started renting the building in 1939. He was known as a well-trained and experienced restaurant owner. He produced a menu that offered a wide range of meals and refreshments to the patrons of the Wright Tavern. The items included a business luncheon for seventy-five cents, Sunday night supper for one dollar and afternoon tea between 3:00 and 5:00 p.m. for fifty cents. He marketed the historic importance of the building as part of his campaign to bring people in. Postcards were prepared and sent around that featured displays within the tavern of historical artifacts. Reports also show that Trumbull Taverns, Inc., a company that ran several inns and taverns, started renting the Wright Tavern in the early 1940s, but this ended in 1944 when Franklin H. Trumbull stepped down as president of the company. It is unclear what happened in the building for the next ten years.

Above: Postcard of the Wright Tavern. *Courtesy of the Concord Free Public Library.*

Middle: Postcard of the Wright Tavern. *Courtesy of the Concord Free Public Library.*

Bottom: Postcard of the Wright Tavern in the early 1920s. *Postcard owned by the Wright Tavern Legacy Trust.*

THE OLD WRIGHT TAVERN, 1747, CONCORD, MASS.

Top: Postcard of the Wright Tavern. *Postcard owned by the Wright Tavern Legacy Trust.*

Middle: Wright Tavern, 1940s. *Postcard owned by the Wright Tavern Legacy Trust.*

Left: Wright Tavern, 1940s. *Postcard owned by the Wright Tavern Legacy Trust.*

Top: Postcard of the Wright Tavern taproom. *Postcard owned by the Wright Tavern Legacy Trust.*

Bottom: The dining room in the Wright Tavern, circa 1930. *Postcard owned by the Wright Tavern Legacy Trust.*

In the mid-1950s, the Wright Tavern stopped being an inn and became a very popular thrift shop. The Women's Union Board of the Trinitarian Congregational Church decided to open a thrift shop in the Wright Tavern where the profits would be contributed to foreign missions. People with means donated goods to the thrift shop, thus allowing poor people to buy high-quality merchandise at significant savings. It was very popular, and by 1958, it had expanded to the entire first floor of the tavern. It became known as the Tri-Con Gift Shop after the Trinitarian Congregational Church. Hundreds of volunteers served in this program, including the children of the women operating the store. It provided many needy people with high-quality material goods and generated over $500 per month for foreign missions. Mary C. Lawrence and Dorris M. Fairburn were some of the original operators of the shop. The shop carried a wide variety of merchandise, including Revolutionary War gifts and small soldiers. They also carried blankets, maps, candlesticks and postcards. Many products were replicas of historical items. This program tapped into Concord's spirit of giving and doing good for others. Often, the daughters of the women who ran the gift shop dressed in 1775-period clothing for the great pleasure of tourists and customers.[141]

During this time, Theodore Jensen rented a small room in the basement as a real estate office. The Tri-Con women sublet part of the kitchen to Milldam Associates, and in 1964, the Walden Guidance Associates rented space on the second floor. The basement had an office that was used by Fan Cabot Larner for her studio for several years before the Concord Chamber of Commerce took over the space. Fan was born in Concord in 1930 and operated many other stores in town (such as Perceptions). In 1998, she was given the Honored Concord Citizens award.

In 1961, the secretary of the U.S. Department of the Interior during Dwight D. Eisenhower's administration, Fred Seaton, designated the Wright Tavern a National Historic Landmark. After a thorough examination of the history of the Wright Tavern, the statement concluded that the tavern was "a historic site of exceptional value in commemorating and illustrating the history of the United States." A plaque hangs on the exterior of this building today, commemorating this important recognition of the Wright Tavern and what happened here in the founding of our country.[142]

The building has continued to be used for various purposes. In the 1970s, the Shaker Workshop sold furniture and operated on the second floor. They moved out in 1975. Abigail's Attic, a swap shop, was a very popular place. Jo Powell's Super Stitch sold yarns and craft materials on

BUILT IN 1747

The WRIGHT TAVERN
KEPT BY AMOS WRIGHT IN 1775

Here met the Committees of the
PROVINCIAL CONGRESS
on the eve of the Revolution
while the larger body sat
in the MEETING HOUSE close by

HEADQUARTERS OF THE MINUTEMEN
IN THE EARY MORNING OF
APRIL 19, 1775

Later that day
Headquarters of the British
under command of
Colonel Smith and Major Pitcairn

Photograph of a plaque granting the Wright Tavern as a National Historical Landmark. *All rights reserved, Wright Tavern Legacy Trust.*

the second floor as well. The many hooks that held her yarns are still in place today.

The Tri-Con Gift Shop closed in 1992. In 1993, the Concord Chamber of Commerce moved into offices in the China Room and the Old Tap Room. Treasurers, a gift and antique shop, moved into other rooms on the first floor. In the early 1990s, Holly Cratsley founded Nashawtuc Architects, which moved into the former dining room and small conference room and later to offices on the second floor. Nashawtuc Architects grew and ultimately rented the second floor of the Wright Tavern for about twenty-five years.

Cratsley, the managing partner, and Josh Bath, the lead project manager, tell of encounters of a spiritual and ghostly variety. They shared several stories that are consistent with sightings at other properties in Concord. One night, a female associate was working late when she suddenly felt her earring start flipping as if someone was touching it. This continued for what must have felt like several minutes until she decided to pack up her things and leave the building. Another of their associates was working in the evening when she felt someone tapping on her shoulder. When she turned, no one was there. This happened a few times until the associate left the building.

On another night, a large mid-twenties male associate was working late. It is reported that he felt things suddenly quiet, and then he felt the presence of someone with him in the room. He turned, but no one was visible. He, too, decided to pack up his work and head for home. Finally, Holly spoke of a problem that kept happening with the employees. Whenever anyone worked at a particular desk that was near one of the fireplaces (they were no longer usable), they would become sick. Some would get the flu, a cold, or something more serious. Holly decided to place a wood cover over the fireplace, thinking a draft could have caused the illnesses. After the flue of the fireplace was blocked, the illnesses stopped. It seems the wood cover helped. These are the only recorded experiences with paranormal sensations in the Wright Tavern.

When First Parish was undergoing a major construction project at the meetinghouse, the ministers and staff occupied offices on the first floor of the Wright Tavern. For many years, the First Parish Youth Group and other First Parish groups used the Wright Tavern for meetings and events. In the basement room, which was the kitchen and bakery ovens for Francis Jarvis, the First Parish children must have had fun painting the old fireplace with a rainbow of colors.

In 1998, First Parish started using the building more extensively. The senior minister, Reverend Gary Smith, along with a colleague minister and member of First Parish, Reverend James Sherblom, started a program called the Wright Tavern Center for Spiritual Renewal. This program held classes in the Wright Tavern to explore applied ethics, offer guided mystic vision quests and host discussions of sacred and ancient texts. Several families contributed the funds needed to open and operate the Wright Tavern Center. They expanded both the awareness and use of this historic building. The programs were open to all. One of the most popular ones was titled "Spiritual Autobiography." This program created a way for people to tell their stories and the journey of their faith throughout their life, with all the mountains and valleys of their experience. The discussions opened new perspectives on how the participants saw and used their faith to guide decisions, especially the difficult ones. The center was active between 1997 and 2003.[143]

The Wright Tavern, under the care and maintenance of First Parish, has had many uses and served many purposes. A time was emerging when the building's historical importance should take greater prominence in its use. Members of First Parish's congregation began to realize that perhaps there should be a different future for the Wright Tavern.

Chapter 10

CREATING THE NEXT CHAPTER
FOR THE WRIGHT TAVERN

In 2014–15, Melvin H. Bernstein, PhD, a member of First Parish and former chair of the American Revolution Roundtable of the Minuteman National Park, encouraged the Standing Committee (the church's governing body), the Trustees of Parish Donations and the congregation of First Parish in Concord to open the Wright Tavern and let it take its rightful place as a major historical landmark in Concord.[144] In 2014, the *Historic Structures Report* was prepared, which documented much of the history of the Wright Tavern and many of the areas that needed extensive repairs or improvements. This was conducted by the Groundroot Preservation Group, Steve Mallory, principal.[145]

Consequently, in 2015–16, First Parish commissioned a group of First Parish and community representatives to explore alternative uses for the Wright Tavern. The study team, known as the Wright Tavern Exploratory Committee, was led by John Boynton, a trustee and member of First Parish. They concluded that the best alternative was to form a relationship with the Concord Museum to use and operate the building. In February 2016, First Parish signed a three-year agreement with the Concord Museum to occupy and provide educational programs and public access to the Wright Tavern.[146]

The Concord Museum was going through a major reconstruction of its facilities and used rooms in the tavern for its offices and programs. They created programs and offered tours and reenactments of important events at the Wright Tavern to school groups and tourists. They also made access improvements for disabled people and outfitted a bathroom to be ADA (Americans with Disabilities Act) compliant. They kept important elements of the first floor untouched and preserved the taproom and meeting rooms. However, due to other business priorities, the Concord Museum did not renew the lease agreement and ceased operations at the tavern in 2019.

Many viewed the relationship between First Parish and the Concord Museum as highly successful. It created great support in the First Parish community for the Wright Tavern to be opened to the public and to participate in the activities of Concord. Nashawtuc Architects continued to use the building when the Concord Museum used the first floor. First Parish groups, including the youth group, used the building for occasional meetings. First Parish has continued to make repairs and improvements to keep the building in good operating condition, but it was essentially closed to the public.

In January 2020, First Parish and the Trustees of Parish Donations decided to form another task force to study and develop a new future for the Wright Tavern. This group was called the Wright Tavern Futures Task Force and included members from the trustees and selected staff members, including Reverend Howard Dana, the senior minister. Other First Parish parishioners (including Mel Bernstein) were included. Tom Wilson, a parishioner with First Parish, a former treasurer of First Parish and a member of the earlier Exploratory Committee, served as the director of the task force.

The task force spent over a year (during the COVID-19 pandemic) examining alternative futures and partnerships for the Wright Tavern. They conducted a thorough engineering and conditions analysis of the building to determine any structural issues or other concerns that need to be addressed before providing public access to the building. Further, they explored potential program and funding partners and held an important community meeting with over twenty guests with particular interest and expertise in the history of the Wright Tavern. These discussions provided the task force with many meaningful perspectives and ideas on a key question: *What should be the future of the Wright Tavern?* During these deliberations, much has been learned about the interest and support within Concord and other communities. It became clear that the future of the Wright Tavern lies in understanding its history within the context of today's challenges and creating opportunities to promote learning and the exploration of ideas—similar to what happened in colonial taverns.

The task force concluded that there was no suitable organization that could easily take over the Wright Tavern and operate it in a way that was consistent

The front of the Wright Tavern. *All rights reserved, Wright Tavern Legacy Trust.*

with the vision for the building. This left the task force and First Parish with a big question: should it return the tavern to offices or embark on a project to restore, rehabilitate and open the building to the public? The latter was clearly the more challenging alternative. However, retaining the current use of the building as offices that are not accessible to the public or provide educational experiences was not acceptable. So, they decided to seek a next chapter for the Wright Tavern that is based on its roots and historical importance.[147]

The Wright Tavern Futures Task Force concluded that certain important principles should guide the future of the Wright Tavern. These are:

1. **The preservation of the Wright Tavern is essential.**
   One of the primary reasons Hoar and Rice gave the Wright Tavern to First Parish was to preserve its historic fabric. First Parish has taken this responsibility very seriously and has, within its means, worked to preserve the core elements of the building. It now needs to take its rightful place in telling the stories of Concord's history and that of Massachusetts and the founding of our country. This building is more than just

another historical building in Concord. It serves as an important original landmark in the founding of the United States.

2. **The tavern, at its roots, is a gathering place for the community to discuss, explore and learn.** It has been an important location for educational programs, discussions, events, reenactments and activities that contribute to the full range of historical sites in and around Concord. The building should have frequent open access to the public and individuals interested in what happened here. After all, for most of its history, the Wright Tavern has been a center for gatherings, discussions, information sharing, educational programs and providing refreshments.

3. **The Wright Tavern should become known as an important birthplace of American independent representative government and serve to promote the principles and ideals of democracy on which this country was founded.** In its beginning, it is where understanding the importance of protecting one's rights took hold. It also stands as a witness to the struggles and cultural changes of Concord and the United States and should support the continued exploration and dialogue of the issues facing our society. That is the role taverns served in colonial America, and it is greatly needed at this time.

4. **The use of the building needs to be financially self-sufficient.** The tavern was given to First Parish in part to help provide additional financial resources to the church. It must not become financially dependent on First Parish, the town, the national parks or other external entities. First Parish has a deep and enduring responsibility for the building and should retain its ownership. The programs and services of the Wright Tavern should make it financially self-sufficient.

5. **To fulfill these principles, we need to create long-term partnerships and collaborative relationships** with other organizations that share our commitment to and responsibility for what the Wright Tavern represents and make the necessary investments to create a truly distinctive attraction in Concord Center. In short, it is essential that we build supportive, integrated relationships with various organizations and sites in order to create a more welcoming community in Concord.

Concord Minutemen in front of the Wright Tavern on Patriot's Day, April 2024. *All rights reserved, Wright Tavern Legacy Trust.*

The task force decided to establish an independent support nonprofit organization (a 501(c)(3) trust organization) entitled the Wright Tavern Legacy Trust to guide the development, use and governance of the Wright Tavern. While it remains the property of First Parish and the responsibility of the Trustees of Parish Donations, the Wright Tavern Legacy Trust Board has overall responsibility for addressing the need to create a new future for the Wright Tavern. They hold a lease for the building and serve to design, develop and manage the renovations to the building, preserving the historic elements, addressing the critical structural issues and creating capabilities for a new future. They will also oversee their programs and services to the community.

The Legacy Trust Board, working with a team of well-recognized historians, preservation and exhibit design architects and others, has developed a new vision for the Wright Tavern that builds on its history and becomes relevant today.

The Wright Tavern will be a welcoming learning center that fosters engagement, inspires the exploration of democracy and provides unique refreshments.

In some ways, this vision is to take the Wright Tavern back to its roots. The core of the Wright Tavern is a place for learning, dialoguing and engaging with others. It is a place where the stories of Concord's current happenings, issues, history and the founding of our country are told. It is a place for meetings, events and reenactments that welcome and facilitate shared experiences. It provides refreshments to our visitors, with coffee/tea in the morning and beer/wine/signature drinks in the afternoon and evening, along with pre-prepared food and snacks throughout the day. The revenue from these space rental fees and refreshments eliminates the need to sell tickets and in turn creates multiple sources of income. Thereby, the Wright Tavern is accessible to all. There is a modest gift shop, so visitors may find an item that reminds them of their experience in the tavern. It is open year-round and ready in the spring/summer/fall for tourist visitors to Concord and provides a rich array of programs and services to the citizens of Concord and surrounding communities throughout the year. The Wright Tavern is run by professionals, and groups may visit the tavern guided by professional interpreters. These services and capabilities will develop as we determine the need and have the financial resources to pay for and implement them over time. In short, the Wright Tavern is an important community asset serving members of our broad community and visitors from throughout the world.

When people come to the Wright Tavern, we want them to hear about the events of the First Massachusetts Provincial Congress and the fears and challenges people faced. We want people to hear the commands of the British Regulars and the intense commitment of the townspeople to be independent. We want people to hear the struggles, challenges and achievements to understand and strengthen human dignity and respect for different points of view. We want those who are engaged in addressing the challenges to democracy to find the Wright Tavern a home, a place for their meetings and engagements, a "tavern" for them in today's world. Finally, we want to share with the world the spirit of the Wright Tavern and our efforts to create a more perfect union through a deeper understanding of the truth and the focus on action that builds community, respect and the preservation of liberty for all people.

This is our vision, this is our mission and this is the framework for our goals. It is time for the Wright Tavern to take its rightful place in telling the stories of Concord's history and the founding of the United States. If not this, what? If not now, when? If not us, who? The Wright Tavern will once again demonstrate the importance and value of taverns in community life. It will provide a unique place for learning, hearing the stories of the past and translating their meaning into today's challenges and be a place to enjoy dialogue and unique refreshments.

This story does not have an ending. The Wright Tavern is entering a new chapter in its life, and hopefully, there will be decades more in which people can experience, learn and enjoy the offerings of this unique building. It is time for the Wright Tavern to enter this next chapter and continue its positive impact on the people of Concord, the United States and the world. It is just that simple and that important.

LIST OF OWNERS AND OCCUPANTS OF THE WRIGHT TAVERN

Year	Owner	Occupant	Description
1747	Ephraim Jones		Tavern
1751	Thomas Munroe		Tavern
1766	Daniel Taylor		Tavern
1774		Amos Wright	Tavern
1775	Samuel Swan	William, John and Thomas Kettell	Tavern, bakery, wig manufacturing
1793	Reuben Brown		Stables keeper
1793	Thomas Safford and Francis Jarvis		Residence and bakery
1795	Francis Jarvis		Bakery
1839	Stephen Jarvis		
		Silas Burges	Livery stables
		James M. Billings	Stables keeper
1853	James M. Billings		Stables keeper
1858	George Prescott and Samuel Staples		

Year	Owner	Occupant	Description
1860	Julius M. Smith		Stables and innkeeper
1864	Daniel H. Wood		Personal residence
1871	Lucy and George Brown		Stables and innkeeper
		John Stacy	Printer, bookbinder, bookstore
		Joe Parks	Tinsmith
		William Wimms	Shoe store
		Frank Potter	Hair balm, Macassar oil
1875	George Brooks		
		Seth Stone	Clandestine beverages
		Otis Penniman	Hotel and poorhouse operator
		Mr. Ward	Unknown
		John Davis	Hotelkeeper
1882	Ebenezer Hoar and Reuben Rice		People's Club
1885	First Parish in Concord		
1894		William Rand	Hotelkeeper
1899		Nellie Tarleton	Hotelkeeper
		John Busch	Hotelkeeper
1910		Charles Willman	Hotelkeeper
1918		Henry Grieme	Hotelkeeper
1925		Mary J. MacDonald	Hotelkeeper
1939		Frank W. Tucker	Hotelkeeper
1955		Women's Union	Tri-Con Gift Shop
1971		Shaker Workshop	Furniture

Year	Owner	Occupant	Description
1975		Abigail's Attic	Swap Shop
		Jo Powell's Super Stitch	Yarn and Craft Shop
1993		Concord Chamber of Commerce	Services to Concord's businesses
1994		Nashawtac Architect	Architectural firm
1998		First Parish	Center for Spiritual Renewal
			First Parish offices
2015		Concord Museum	Offices and tourism
2019		Compass Real Estate	Real estate
2021		Wright Tavern Legacy Trust	

NOTES

Chapter 2

1. Sherblom, "Concord Stories."
2. Pluralism Project, "Native Traditions in Boston."
3. Wallenfeldt, "Massachusetts Bay Colony."
4. Sherblom, "Concord Stories."
5. Ancestor Biographies, "Timothy Wheeler."
6. Cole, "Analysis of Wright Tavern," 1.
7. Tolman, *Wright's Tavern*, 11.
8. Cole, "Analysis of Wright Tavern," 1.
9. Tolman, *Wright's Tavern*, 15.
10. "History of First Parish," www.FirstParish.org.
11. First Parish in Concord Record, 1695-2014, Vault A30, Unit A-1, Concord Free Public Library.
12. Sherblom, "Concord Stories," ch. 4.
13. Conroy, *In Public Houses*.
14. Sherblom, "Concord Stories."
15. History Trekker, "Daily Life of the American Colonies."
16. Sabin, *New England Tavern*.
17. Wheeler, *Concord: Climate for Freedom*.
18. Struzinski, "Tavern in Colonial America."
19. "Wright Tavern—Past, Present and Future," presentation at the Minuteman Visitors Center, May 15, 2015.
20. Sherblom, "Concord Stories."

Chapter 3

21. Shattuck, *History of the Town of Concord*.
22. Ibid.
23. Cole, "Analysis of Wright Tavern," 4.
24. Find a Grave, "Amos Wright."
25. Tolman, *Wright's Tavern*, 23.
26. Nelson, *Concord*, 39.

Chapter 4

27. Britannica, "American Revolution."
28. Beck, *Igniting the American Revolution*, 31.
29. Fischer, *Paul Revere's Ride*, 39.
30. Gross, *Minutemen and Their World*, 53.
31. Ibid.
32. Ibid., 65.
33. Unger, *John Hancock*, 106.
34. Gross, *Minutemen and Their World*, 72.
35. Ibid., 57.
36. Norton, *1774*, 271.
37. Unger, *John Hancock*, 184.
38. Gross, *Minutemen and Their World*, 134.
39. Circular letter of April 20, 1773, in Krollenberg, Growth, 261, as sourced from Unger, *John Hancock*, 185.
40. Sherblom, "Concord Stories," ch. 4.
41. Nelson, *Concord*, 31.

Chapter 5

42. Ibid.
43. Fischer, *Paul Revere's Ride*, 82.
44. Ibid.
45. Beck, *Igniting the American Revolution*, 101.
46. Fischer, *Paul Revere's Ride*, 89.
47. Ibid., 98.
48. Sherblom, "Concord Stories," ch. 4.

49. Ibid.
50. Gross, *Minutemen and Their World*, 115.
51. Klein, "Midnight Ride of William Dawes."
52. Fischer, *Paul Revere's Ride*, 112.
53. Gross, *Minutemen and Their World*, 116.
54. Fischer, *Paul Revere's Ride*, 88–90.
55. Ibid., 123.
56. Wheeler, *Concord: Climate for Freedom*.
57. Gross, *Minutemen and Their World*, 146.
58. Fischer, *Paul Revere's Ride*, 194–97.
59. Gross, *Minutemen and Their World*, 147.
60. Ibid., 120.
61. Fischer, *Paul Revere's Ride*, 204.

Chapter 6

62. Beck, *Igniting the American Revolution*, 137.
63. Amos Barrett in the letter of Reverend Henry Ture (1900), from Library of Congress, *Journal and Letters of Rev. Henry Ture of Hampstead, New Hampshire*, 31.
64. Keyes, *Brief History of Concord*, ch. 43.
65. Beck, *Igniting the American Revolution*, 159.
66. Wheeler, *Concord: Climate for Freedom*, 129.
67. Tourtellot, *Lexington and Concord*.
68. Gross, *Minutemen and Their World*, 148.
69. Beck, *Igniting the American Revolution*, 162.
70. Bell, "Reviewing Thomas Nichols's Case."
71. Gross, *Minutemen and Their World*, 122.
72. Shattuck, *History of the Town of Concord*, 108–9.
73. Nelson, *Concord*, 30.
74. Ibid., 33.
75. Ripley, *History of the Fight*, 19.
76. Tourtellot, *Lexington and Concord*, 157.
77. Wheeler, *Concord: Climate for Freedom*, 129.
78. Gross, *Minutemen and Their World*, 152.
79. Fischer, *Paul Revere's Ride*, 208.
80. Beck, *Igniting the American Revolution*, 130.
81. Gross, *Minutemen and Their World*, 125.

82. "Concord's North Bridge," a paper by the Minuteman National Park Service.
83. Beck, *Igniting the American Revolution*, 270.
84. Gross, *Minutemen and Their World*, 125.
85. Ibid., 156.
86. Beck, *Igniting the American Revolution*, 175.
87. Tourtellot, *Lexington and Concord*, 167.
88. Gross, *Minutemen and Their World*, 120.
89. Fischer, *Paul Revere's Ride*, 219.
90. Ibid., 232.
91. Wheeler, *Concord: Climate for Freedom*.
92. Busch, *An Historic Tour*, 28.

Chapter 7

93. Fischer, *Paul Revere's Ride*, 219.
94. Gross, *Minutemen and Their World*, 134.
95. Tolman, *Wright's Tavern*, 20.
96. Ibid.
97. Gross, *Minutemen and Their World*, 213.
98. Ibid., 215.
99. Wheeler, *Concord: Climate for Freedom*, 172.
100. "Middlesex Hotel Story," Special Collections paper in the Concord Free Public Library.
101. American Battlefield Trust, "Biography of Daniel Shays."
102. History.com, "Shays's Rebellion."
103. Gross, *Minutemen and Their World*, 187.
104. "Deacon Francis Jarvis Papers, 1797–1825," Special Collections, Concord Public Library, Vault A45, Unit 3.
105. Tolman, *Wright's Tavern*, 21.
106. Sherblom, "Concord Stories."
107. Gross, *Transcendentalists and Their World*, 31.
108. Ibid.
109. Sherblom, "Concord Stories," ch. 5.
110. Brandon, *Lafayette*, 159.
111. Jarvis, "Memoir of Francis Jarvis," 30.
112. Groundroot Preservation Group, *Historic Structure Report*, 10.

Chapter 8

113. Gross, *Transcendentalists and Their World*, 188.
114. Sherblom, "Concord Stories," ch. 5.
115. Gross, *Transcendentalists and Their World*, 333.
116. Ibid., 336–37.
117. Ibid., 358–59.
118. Robbins House, "Ellen Garrison."
119. Ibid.
120. Shattuck, *History of the Town of Concord*, 105.
121. Nelson, *Concord*, 69.
122. Gross, *Transcendentalists and Their World*, 376–77.
123. Nelson, *Concord*, 71.
124. Sherblom, "Concord Stories," ch. 5.
125. Nelson, *Concord*, 78.
126. Sherblom, "Concord Stories," ch. 5.
127. Groundroot Preservation Group, *Historic Structure Report*, 10.
128. Sherblom, "Concord Stories," ch. 5; Gross, *Transcendentalists and Their World*, 224.
129. Groundroot Preservation Group, *Historic Structure Report*, 11.
130. Concord Grape Association.
131. Sherblom, "Concord Stories," ch. 5.
132. Interview transcript of Donald Prentiss, a descendant of Otis Pennyman; the interview was conducted on April 20, 2011, and is part of the Concord Free Public Library Oral History Project.
133. Groundroot Preservation Group, *Historic Structure Report*, 12.
134. *Concord Enterprise*, July 8, 1892, 9.
135. Tolman, *Wright's Tavern*, 20.
136. Ibid., 35.

Chapter 9

137. Sherblom, "Concord Stories," ch. 6.
138. Groundroot Preservation Group, *Historic Structure Report*, 12.
139. Peter Mitchell is a long-standing member of First Parish in Concord, and this tale was told to the author during a casual conversation.
140. Sherblom, "Concord Stories," ch. 6.

141. The interview transcript of Mary C. Lawrence (with her daughter Sara Lawrence), conducted on November 4, 2015; this interview is part of the Concord Free Public Library Oral History Project collection.
142. "Wright's Tavern—Massachusetts," National Survey of Historic Sites and Buildings.
143. Interview transcript with Reverend Gary Smith, minister, First Parish Unitarian Universalist Church, conducted on August 22, 2001, as part of the Concord Free Public Library Oral History Project.

Chapter 10

144. Bernstein, "Concord's Best Kept Secret."
145. Groundroot Preservation Group, *Historic Structure Report*.
146. "Report of the Wright Tavern Exploratory Committee."
147. See "Meeting Minutes and Presentations" by the Wright Tavern Futures task force, contained in the files managed by the Wright Tavern Legacy Trust.

BIBLIOGRAPHY

Alden, John R. *General Gage in America: Being Principally a History of His Role in the American Revolution*. Baton Rouge: Louisiana State University Press, 1948.

American Battlefield Trust. "Biography of Daniel Shays." www.battlefields. org/learn/biographies/daniel-shays.

Ancestor Biographies. "Captain of the Concord Milita—Timothy Wheeler." ancestorbios.blogspot.com/search?q=timothy+wheeler.

Ancestry.com.

Baker, Doug. *Historical Highlights: First Parish and Its Meeting Houses*. Concord, MA: First Parish in Concord, n.d.

Beck, Derek W. *Igniting the American Revolution: 1773–1775*. Naperville, IL: Sourcebooks, 2015.

Bell, J.L. "Reviewing Thomas Nichols's Case." Boston 1775. www. boston1775.blogspot.com.

———. *The Road to Concord: How Four Stolen Cannon Ignited the Revolutionary War*. Yardley, PA: Westholme Publishing, 2016.

Bernstein, Melvin. "Concord's Best Kept Secret—The Wright Tavern." *Concord Journal*, March 12, 2015.

———. "Wright Tavern Confronts an Uncertain Future." *Concord Journal*, October 3, 2019.

Brandon, W.W., ed. *Lafayette: Guest of the Nation*. Vol. 1. Oxford Historical Press, 1950.

Britannica. "American Revolution." www.britannica.com/event/American-Revolution.

Busch, John J. *A Historic Tour: A Pilgrimage to the Birthplace of American Liberty and the Homes of Our Foremost Authors*. Boston, Hudson Printing Company, 1913.

Cole, John. "Analysis of Wright Tavern History and Architecture." Report, Ipswich, MA, May 17, 1989.

Concord Grape Association. www.concordgrape.org.

Conroy, David. *In Public Houses: Drink and the Revolution of Authority in Massachusetts*. Chapel Hill: University of North Carolina Press, 1995.

Curran, Victor. "Reuban Brown: The Lieutenant's Legacy." *Discover Concord*, Fall 2022.

Find a Grave. "Amos Wright." www.findagrave.com/memorial/133387570/amos-wright.

Fischer, David Hackett. *Paul Revere's Ride*. Oxford, UK: Oxford University Press, 1994.

French, Allen. *Historic Concord & the Lexington Fight*. Concord, MA: Friends of the Concord Free Public Library, 1992.

Gross, Robert. *The Minutemen and Their World*. New York: Hill and Wang Publishers, updated edition 2022.

———. *The Transcendentalists and Their World*. New York: Picador Publisher, 2021.

Groundroot Preservation Group. *Historic Structure Report: The Wright Tavern*. 2014.

History.com. "Shays' Rebellion." www.history.com/topics/early-us/shays-rebellion, June 20, 2023.

The History Trekker. "Daily Life of the American Colonies: The Role of the Tavern in Society." www.thehistorytrekker.com/travel-photographer/new-england/daily-life-of-the-american-colonies-the-role-of-the-tavern-in-society.

Hudson, Alfred Sereno. *History of Concord, Massachusetts*. N.p.: Jazzybee Verlag publisher, 2018.

Jarvis, Edward. "Memoir of Francis Jarvis." *Memoirs of Members of the Social Circle in Concord*. Cambridge, MA: Riverside Press, 1888.

Keyes, John. *A Brief History of Concord*. Philadelphia: J.W. Lewis & Co., 1890.

Klein, Christopher. "The Midnight Ride of William Dawes." History.com, April 18, 2012.

Land deed transfers, research conducted by Beth van Duzer.

"Massachusetts Provincial Congress." www.Encyclopedia.com.

Nelson, Elizabeth. *Concord: Stories to Be Told.* Beverly, MA: Commonwealth Editions, 2002.

Norton, Mary Beth. *1774: The Long Year of Revolution.* New York: Vintage Books, 2020.

Pluralism Project of Harvard University. "Native Traditions in Boston." pluralism.org/native-traditions-in-boston.

Provincial Congress Collections. Massachusetts Archives.

"Report of the Wright Tavern Exploratory Committee." February 22, 2016.

Ripley, Ezra. *History of the Fight.* Concord, MA: Allen & Atwill, 1827.

Robbins House. "Ellen Garrison." robbinshouse.org/story/ellen-garrison-jackson.

Sabin, Douglas, prep. *The New England Tavern: A General Study.* Minuteman National Parks, October 1982.

Shattuck, Lemuel. *History of the Town of Concord.* Middlesex County, MA: Russell, Odiorne, and Company, 1835.

Sherblom, James. "Concord Stories." Pre-published manuscript, with author's permission.

Struzinski, Steven. "The Tavern in Colonial America." *Gettysburg Historical Journal* 1, no. 7 (2002).

Tolman, George. *Wright's Tavern.* Concord, MA: Concord Antiquarian Society, December 2, 1901.

Tourtellot, Arthur B. *Lexington and Concord: The Beginning of the War of the American Revolution.* New York: W.W. Norton & Company, 1959.

Unger, Harlow Giles. *John Hancock: Merchant King and American Patriot.* New York: John Wiley & Sons, 2000.

Wallenfeldt, Jeff. "Massachusetts Bay Colony." Encyclopedia Britannica, April 2024.

Wheeler, Ruth. *Concord: Climate for Freedom.* Concord, MA: Concord Antiquarian Society, 1967.

"Wright's Tavern—Massachusetts." National Survey of Historic Sites and Buildings, by the Department of the Interior, January 20, 1961.

Wroth, L. Kinvin, et al., eds. *Province in Rebellion: A Documentary History of the Founding of the Commonwealth of Massachusetts, 1774–1775.* Cambridge, MA: Harvard University Press, 1975.

ABOUT THE AUTHOR

Tom Wilson is the chair of the board for the Wright Tavern Legacy Trust in Concord, Massachusetts. The trust's mission is to transform the Wright Tavern through restoration, preservation and renewal into a community gathering place, a center for the exploration of democracy and an immersive learning museum.

Tom has had a distinguished career in management consulting, business and writing. He is the founder and CEO of the Wilson Group, which helps clients implement their strategy and build their desired culture by aligning their total compensation and reward programs with their key drivers of success

Tom is the author of three books: *Innovative Reward Systems for the Changing Workplace* (McGraw Hill), *Rewards That Drive High Performance* (AMACOM) and *Next Stage: In Your Retirement, Create the Life You Want* (Balboa Press). The latter book provides an invaluable resource on transitioning from an active career to the period of life often called "retirement."

Tom holds a bachelor's degree from Southern Methodist University and a master's degree from Vanderbilt Owen School of Management. He lives in Concord, Massachusetts, with his wife, Martha, and regularly hikes the trails of Concord with his dog, Ollie.

Tom can be reached at tom@wrighttavern.org.